MACMILLAN MODERN DRAMATISTS

Macmillan Modern Dramatists

Series Editors: *Bruce King* and *Adele King*

Published titles

Further titles in preparation

ATHOL FUGARD

Dennis Walder

Lecturer in Literature
Open University

MACMILLAN

First published 1984

Published by
Higher and Further Education Division
MACMILLAN PUBLISHERS LTD
Houndmills, Basingstoke, Hampshire RG21 2XS
and London
Companies and representatives
throughout the world

Typeset by Wessex Typesetters Ltd
Frome, Somerset

Printed in Great Britain by
Camelot Press Ltd,
Southampton

British Library Cataloguing in Publication Data
Walder, Dennis
Athol Fugard. – (Macmillan modern dramatists)
1. Fugard, Athol – Criticism and interpretation
I. Title
822   PR9369.3.F8Z/
ISBN 0–333–30903–0
ISBN 0–333–30904–9 (pbk)

Contents

List of Plates

1. Athol and Sheila Fugard with the African Theatre Workshop, Sophiatown, Johannesburg, 1958/9. Photograph © Jurgen Schadeberg.
2. Athol Fugard directing Zakes Mokae as Blackie in *Nongogo*, Johannesburg, 1959. Photograph © Jurgen Schadeberg.
3. Zach (Zakes Mokae) threatens Morrie (Ian Bannen) in *The Blood Knot* at the New Arts Theatre, London, 1963. Photograph © David Sim/*Observer*.
4. Janet Suzman and Ben Kingsley in the RSC production of *Hello and Goodbye* at The Place, London (later transferred to The King's Head, London), 1973. Photograph © Donald Cooper.
5. Athol Fugard as the servile Boesman in the film version of *Boesman and Lena*, directed by Ross Devenish, 1974. Photograph © Blue Water Production.
6. Athol Fugard rehearsing two Serpent Players (Mike Ngxcolo and George Mnci) in *Antigone*, Port Elizabeth, 1965. Photograph © Jurgen Schadeberg.

Acknowledgements

At present there is little available on Fugard and his plays, apart from reviews, interviews, somewhat fugitive critical articles and dissertations – and one book-length collection of some of this material. But I have drawn on meetings, interviews and correspondence with the playwright, his actors, actresses, collaborators and friends. I am grateful to them all. I should like especially to thank Athol Fugard himself for his generous responsiveness to enquiries; I should also like to thank Brian Astbury, Mary Benson, Richard Brain, Yvonne Bryceland, Ross Devenish, Nadine Gordimer, Stephen Gray, Yvonne Illum, Bonisile (John) Kani, Mike Kirkwood, James Lodge, Don MacLennan, Mary MacLeod, Matsemela Manaka, Maishe Maponya, John Matshikiza, Alastair Niven, Richard Rive, Barney Simon, Tony Trew and Marius Weyers. I am of course responsible for any errors of fact or judgement. The staff of the National English Literary Museum, Grahamstown, which houses the major public collection of Fugard material, provided friendly and attentive service, as did the

Acknowledgements

Centre for South African Theatre Research in Pretoria, South Africa. The Open University paid for travel and research.

Note

The dates given with the first mention of a play are the dates of first performance.

Editors' Preface

The *Macmillan Modern Dramatists* is an international series of introductions to major and significant nineteenth- and twentieth-century dramatists, movements and new forms of drama in Europe, Great Britain, America and new nations such as Nigeria and Trinidad. Besides new studies of great and influential dramatists of the past, the series includes volumes on contemporary authors, recent trends in the theatre and on many dramatists, such as writers of farce, who have created theatre 'classics' while being neglected by literary criticism. The volumes in the series devoted to individual dramatists include a biography, a survey of the plays, and detailed analysis of the most significant plays, along with discussion, where relevant, of the political, social, historical and theatrical context. The authors of the volumes, who are involved with theatre as playwrights, directors, actors, teachers and critics, are concerned with the plays as theatre and discuss such matters as performance, character interpretation and staging, along with themes and contexts.

BRUCE KING
ADELE KING

1
Introduction

Sunday is not generally a day when anything happens in South Africa. But on Sunday, 3 September 1961, in a cramped, unventilated room on the third floor of an abandoned factory in Eloff Street, Johannesburg, something did happen. A new South African play was performed in which, for the first time, a white man and a black man appeared together on stage. And for nearly four hours the two held their invited, multiracial audience spellbound. Traffic noises drifted up from the front of the building, drumming and chanting from an African miners' hostel at the back penetrated the empty egg-boxes pinned to the windows. But the journalists, theatre people and assorted friends who packed the new 'Rehearsal Room' of the African Music and Drama Association in Dorkay House were gripped as never before by a passionate duet which probed and revealed the feelings associated with that perennial South African subject – race.

The play was *The Blood Knot*, by Athol Fugard; the actors, 'Arrie Potgieter' (Fugard himself, using his maternal grandfather's name) and Zakes Mokae. Fugard also directed, using Barney Simon as a 'third eye'. When the performers awoke the next morning, the event was all over the newspapers. Oliver Walker devoted his entire 'Arts and Entertainment' column in the *Star* (usually dominated by fulsome accounts of productions such as *The Amorous Prawn*) to praise for the new work. On 8 November, cut to two-and-a-half hours, the play reopened under professional management at the Intimate Theatre, Johannesburg. Approval was unanimous, and a tour practically sold out before it began. From the barely known author of two 'township' plays – *No-Good Friday* (1958) and *Nongogo* (1959) – Athol Fugard had become a national figure, virtually overnight. Successful production and publication in London and New York followed in due course and, slowly but surely, an international reputation. With twelve plays (including joint ventures such as *Sizwe Bansi Is Dead*, 1973) currently in print, and his latest – *'Master Harold' . . . and the boys* (1982) – a phenomenal success both at home and abroad, Fugard may be said to have become a major modern playwright. His plays now command an audience whenever and wherever they are performed. He has transformed the limitations of his South African background into theatre of great power and lasting implication.

Fugard's theatre is radical, even extreme; but this is in response to an extreme situation. He lives in a society familiar the world over for its unique system of racial oppression. Brutality and degradation are, of course, to be found elsewhere than in South Africa. But there is a level and quality of humiliation, suffering and despair present in the lives of millions of ordinary South Africans – mostly, but not exclusively black – which demands recognition. Fugard's plays help obtain that recognition. His plays make us aware not only of the South African dimension of man's inhumanity to man, but also of the secret pain we all inflict upon each other in the private recesses of our closest relationships. His works all focus upon two or three people inextricably entangled by the ties of blood, love or friendship. He shows them struggling to survive in an arbitrary, bleak and almost meaningless world. This does not mean his plays lack feeling: on the contrary, they are filled with anger and compassion. It is his great strength to move us deeply by showing the plight of ordinary people caught up in the meshes of social, political, racial and even religious forces which they are unable to understand or control. It is his weakness that he cannot reflect upon or analyse these forces himself. He is like the actor in Brecht's *Messingkauf Dialogues* who provokes 'all sorts of passions, but a passion for argument – oh no'. For Fugard, the message is too urgent. This does not mean that he is simply a propagandist – although propaganda has its place. What it does mean is that there is a characteristic intensity of effect gained by his work, an effect of painful, shared awareness, which it is perhaps uniquely possible to create in the theatre. And Fugard is, above all, in the clichéd phrase, a man of the theatre. As actor, director and playwright, he is obsessed with the idea that what he has to say can only be said indirectly, as an *image*, embodied in the 'living moment' on stage.

He began by going back to the so-called 'Method' school, according to which actors authenticate their roles by finding in them some relation to their own experience. In the – mainly American – development of this approach, the tendency has been to rely on naturalistic performances of pre-existing texts, constructed according to the familiar hierarchy of writer, director, producer and actor. But, although naturalism remains an important thread in Fugard's work, he has moved away from it, towards a more characteristically modern, symbolic realm. Surface reality, or the 'facts' of everyday experience, are never entirely ignored; but the suggestive 'sub-text' is often more important. He is fundamentally opposed to the parochial consumer art with which most Western playgoers are, alas, all too familiar: that mode of drama which pushes the performers into a well-lit picture frame behind a proscenium arch, where they converse with one another according to a given script, while the audience looks on passively. Like such influential and innovative directors as Peter Brook and Jerzy Grotowski, whose work and ideas (especially Grotowski's) have been important for him, Fugard is inspired and sustained by the actuality of performance, by live actors before a live audience, 'flesh and blood, sweat, the human voice, real pain, real time'. For him, as for that great progenitor of 'living theatre' in our day, Antonin Artaud (1896–1948), the trappings of the institutionalised, illusionistic theatre – buildings, props, costumes, lighting and so on – only interest in so far as they aid the primary function of drama: to find the 'truth' of the 'living moment'.[1]

The living moment in a Fugard play tends to emerge as the climax of a shifting pattern of emotions of gradually increasing strength, a moment of revelation, expressed as an image. Words are only a part of what he defines – in terms borrowed from Ezra Pound – as the 'image': 'the presentation of a psychological and emotional complex in an instant of time'. Any script which has not stood the test of production is 'provisional' and 'rough'; and, whatever else may change during workshops, rehearsals or production, he does not concede 'any alteration with the central image – once that happens you have a new play'.[2] Most of Fugard's plays begin life as, and finally focus on, one central image or cluster of images. The climax of *Hello and*

Goodbye (1965), for instance, occurs when Johnnie, unable to leave home and face life, takes up his father's crutches: 'Why not? It solves problems. Let's face it, a man on his own two legs is a shaky proposition.' A chilling and disturbing moment: the crippling inadequacies of family life are exposed simultaneously with – on the deeper, sub-textual level – the failure of the 'poor white' Afrikaner to come to terms with his past. And, when, in *Sizwe Bansi Is Dead*, the central character sits frozen in a grotesquely comic pose, a 'studio' cigarette balanced nonchalantly in one hand, his own pipe gripped firmly in the other, the photographer's studio backdrop of city skyscrapers behind him, while a beatific smile spreads slowly across his features . . . the image sums up the truth of his life: Robert/Sizwe is a naïve dreamer, a simple man who wishes to survive with dignity, but it is a wish as far out of reach as those skyscrapers, for a black man in his situation.

The dramatic impact of the living moments in Fugard's plays represent a stage on a journey, when the 'external story' he has found in the lives and circumstances of those around him coincides with his own 'inner dynamic'. He is engaged in a 'slow trek through the detours of art', as it was put by a writer he resembles as well as admires, Albert Camus (1913–60) – a trek to rediscover 'those two or three great and simple images in whose presence his heart first opened'.[3] Without the coincidence of 'external' and 'internal' in an image, Fugard's plays could not be written. For all the 'external', even documentary detail of his work, it always demonstrates a deeply personal concern for the fate of the 'ordinary', anonymous, *little* people with whom he most closely identifies. The opening entry of Camus's notebooks reads, 'I must bear witness. When I see things clearly, I have only one thing to say. It is in this life of poverty, among these vain or humble people, that I have

assuage
conscience ?

most certainly touched what I feel is the true meaning of
life.' Similarly for Fugard: his 'true meaning', he says in *his*
notebooks, his 'life's work', is 'just to witness' as 'truthfully'
as he can 'the nameless and destitute' of his 'one little
corner of the world'.[4] For Camus, that 'corner' lay in North
Africa, among the white *colons* and their despised local
helotry; for Fugard it is the Eastern Cape region of South
Africa, among the 'poor whites', the 'Coloureds' (mixed
race) and, occasionally, members of the subject African
majority. Like Camus, Fugard belongs by birth and upbringing to the relatively underprivileged sector of the
white group which rules his country, a lower middle-class,
verging on 'poor white', group, which tends to provide the
strongest anti-black feelings and which therefore considers
him a 'traitor' for turning against their own apparent
interests. Camus was led to exile; Fugard insists on staying,
believing that only while living where he is can he testify to
the lives of those around him, the disinherited and the lost –
whether it is Morris and Zach, the two 'Coloured' brothers
of *The Blood Knot*, or Sizwe Bansi, or Johnnie, or Milly
(*People Are Living There*, 1968) or *Boesman and Lena*
(1969) – or even, in her way, which is the way of insanity,
Gladys Bezuidenhout, the bus-driver's wife in *A Lesson
from Aloes* (1978). When Fugard leaves these 'small'
people, as in *Dimetos* (1975), and attempts to create and
study a character who is heroic, even mythical, he loses his
way, becoming abstract and unsympathetic.

Yet, like other modern artists (including Camus, whose
notebooks provided the story of Dimetos), Fugard fre-
quently returns to the mythical – or, at least, to the early
myths of the classical Greek era, the bloody family feuds
dramatised by Aeschylus, Sophocles and Euripides. Hence
the little-known work entitled *Orestes* (1971); hence the
use of *Antigone* in *The Island* (1973). He feels he is

touching on the basic drives which motivate us all, and so is naturally drawn to the most powerful and lasting embodiment of them, in the Greek drama. Is there then no closer tradition which might have provided him with a source of inspiration? Where is the South African tradition?

There is no systematic or comprehensive account of drama in South Africa – much less of South African literature as a whole, incorporating (as it should) the various strands, oral and written, in African as well as European languages, going back to the earliest times. The only half-decent book on the subject, Stephen Gray's *Southern African Literature* (1979) begins by confessing the impossibility of his task: he refers to the fact that by the late 1960s at least half South Africa's English-speaking writers of all colours had been expelled from the country into 'an international diaspora' with the result that South African literature in English had split so 'irremediably and bitterly into two' that it only makes sense to talk of 'two distinct literatures at present'. And this is while focusing only on South African writing *in English*. Gray goes on to identify what he calls an 'archipelago' of literatures, somehow associated merely by being where they are. He omits not only the writers to whom he cannot have access as a scholar working in South Africa, but also the larger framework which might make sense of his material: that is, *history*. But, as Dan Jacobson once remarked, a colonial culture is precisely one in which the sense of history is 'deficient'. This deficiency means that the enmities engendered by the conditions which first brought the colony into existence tend to be regarded 'as so many given, unalterable facts of life, phenomena of nature, as little open to human change or question as the growth of leaves in spring'.[5] Typically, the members of such a culture delude themselves into believing that things have always been the way they are, and always will be. South Africa is a good example: it is a fragmented ex-colonial culture; and it is a culture in which the potential for unity and integration has not only been resisted by the dominant white minority, but has been corrupted according to an ideology which emphasises and exploits difference, so as to manipulate and control the vast majority. Even apart from the specific effects of apartheid laws – of censorship, of bannings, imprisonment and exile – there is a history of division and isolation which has made it difficult, if not impossible, for people to know what is going on in their own country. For writers and artists, this leads to the common feeling that they are operating in a vacuum.

When Fugard was asked what dramatists he had met during the early years of his career in the 1950s, he replied, 'There were none around.'[6] In fact there was taking place at the time a so-called 'renaissance' of English drama, including plays by Alan Paton, James Ambrose Brown and Lewis Sowden – the last of whom wrote a play, *Kimberley Train* (1958), which anticipates the subject of *The Blood Knot*. But in terms of quality and relevance Fugard may seem right to have presumed 'There were none around.' On the other hand, there was also a less well documented or known 'renaissance' in the urban black 'townships', an upsurge of popular theatre, of song and dance, of satire and jazz, which white entrepreneurs in Johannesburg at least were aware of, and which became more familiar with the emergence in 1959 of the jazz opera *King Kong*. *King Kong* was essentially urban, and should not be confused with such dubious successors as *uMabatha* (1970) or *Ipi Tombi* (1973), all-black musical productions designed by their white managements to present the impression of black South Africans as a crowd of smiling, dancing, bare-breasted rural illiterates. The last decade has, in fact, seen a flood of 'township' drama, ranging from the sensational accounts of everyday urban life purveyed by Gibson Kente and Sam Mhangwani (the latter's unpublished *Unfaithful Wife* remains a hit after twenty years) to the more serious, politically committed work of writers such as Maishe Maponya (*The Hungry Earth*, 1979) and Matsemela Manaka (*Egoli*, 1980) – to name only a few from Soweto alone.

Fugard has acknowledged his debt to black *performers*: those first befriended in Sophiatown, the multiracial Johannesburg ghetto, in the late fifties, and whose talents and experiences were embodied in his first full-length plays, *No-Good Friday* and *Nongogo*; as well as those who came to him from New Brighton, Port Elizabeth, in 1963 to form the Serpent Players, a remarkable group whose collaborative work led to (amongst other plays) *Sizwe Bansi Is Dead* and *The Island*. Fugard's own influence upon 'township' theatre is recognised and is continuing. Playwrights in the townships have had to learn a tough lesson in survival, a lesson they articulate in a variety of forms, using whatever means they can – including the aid of those few, such as Fugard and writer–director Barney Simon, willing and able to 'cross over' from the white side to offer the knowledge and experience to which they have privileged access. But such contact barely deflects the pressures of the situation. Dramatists still feel they must start from scratch, unable to draw on the fragmented, unknown or unacknowledged traditions of their own country.

So it is not altogether surprising that Fugard's acknowledged mentors should not be South African. One of the few playwrights to whom he admits he owes anything is Samuel Beckett – an allegiance confirmed by his small casts, sparse sets, flat, seemingly pointless dialogue and inconsequential plots. But, even if some such influence can be traced, Fugard's plays are all ultimately derived 'from life and from encounters with real people', as he put it in the Introduction to his published notebooks. These notebooks reveal the secret, slow and painful germination of his plays over many years, culminating in *'Master Harold'* . . . *and the boys* – which, based upon an incident in his adolescence, has had the longest incubation of them all, no doubt because it is the most personal, and has been the most difficult to expose. Evidently *'Master Harold'* was a cathartic experience for him; and so it is for his audiences, too. There is nothing 'literary' about this: it is primarily a matter of transferring emotions, of arousing in us a powerful and deep emotional awareness, which burns into our consciousness the imagery of a group of individual human beings caught within the conflicting tensions of their specific situation. The nature of their relationships suggests the profound forces at work in their society; the characters in his plays are revealed struggling to survive with some shred of dignity the almost intolerable burden of suffering imposed upon them by an apparently irresistible fate. If this seems to suggest an endorsement of suffering, of passivity in the face of oppression, that seems to be true; but it is not the whole truth. Fugard's work also contains a potential for subversion, a potential which, I would suggest, is the hallmark of great art, and which qualifies his best work to be called great.

Art is often called revolutionary if it represents a radical quality in style or technique; but there is a more important sense in which it can be revolutionary – or, as I would prefer to put it, subversive. This lies in its potential to undermine the status quo, a potential revealed in its tendency to make us realise that things need not be the way they have been, or the way they are. If racialism and exploitation seem natural as 'the growth of leaves in

spring', then it is in the capacity of art to show us that this is
not so. As Brecht said, to make the ordinary extraordinary.
Before a word was uttered in that first performance of *The
Blood Knot* in September 1961, the audience was
presented with a curious sight: a pale-skinned man, shab-
bily dressed (Morris, played by Fugard), coming in and
setting about preparing a footbath, timing his actions
(which are evidently routine) by means of an old alarm-
clock; an equally shabby man, of African appearance
(Zach, played by Mokae) but wearing a greatcoat and
obviously returning from a hard day's work, then enters,
and makes a great show of being surprised at the footbath,
testing the water with one toe, and so on, before finally and
luxuriously resting his calloused feet in it. In that 'living
moment', that 'image', a relationship was suggested which
thrilled the audience with disturbing implications: revealing a white man behaving like a housekeeper, a servant, to a
black. The relationship at the centre of the structure of
South African society was being subverted before their
eyes. *The Blood Knot* went on to reveal that the two were
mixed-race brothers, outcasts tormented by the fact that
one of them was more 'European' in appearance than the
other; and the alternating pattern of dominance and
dependence between them which this generated in a
racialist society. But it is the lasting, subversive resonance
of that initial image and the variations upon it which follow
that provide the play with the possibility of its continuing
power and relevance.

All Fugard's plays approximate to the same basic model,
established by *The Blood Knot*: a small cast of 'marginal'
characters is presented in a passionately close relationship
embodying the tensions current in their society, the whole
first performed by actors directly involved in its creation, in
a makeshift, 'fringe' or 'unofficial' venue. This is 'poor

theatre', although less as a matter of theory (Grotowski's *Towards a Poor Theatre* only came to Fugard in 1970) than as a matter of preferred practice. With few resources and impelled to operate under rough, workshop conditions, relying on actors to impart their own experiences, Fugard has always worked outside the conventional, mainstream theatre, implicitly challenging by his conditions of production the prevailing assumptions about theatre – i.e. that it is a form of packaged entertainment which confirms the status quo. Despite the subsequent, inevitable assimilation of his most well-known works into that mainstream theatre, as far as he is concerned all that the theatre, *his* theatre needs is (as he put it at the time of *The Blood Knot*, and has repeated ever since)

> the actor and the stage, the actor *on* the stage. Around him is space, to be filled and defined by movement and gesture; around him is also silence to be filled with meaning, using words and sounds, and at moments when all else fails him, including the words, the silence itself.[7]

This helps explain his reliance upon his chosen actors, as well as his determination always to have a controlling hand in the production of all his plays; the end product is not so much a written text, which may only be a record of a performance, but an existential moment, in a particular place at a particular time. What his plays mean is determined less by their written words than by the total conditions of performance. This became especially important to him when, under the impact of the ideas of Grotowski and the workshop practice developed with the Serpent Players, he attempted his most 'extreme excursion' into radical communication by means of image and gesture, rather than pre-established text: *Orestes*, which defies translation into a script, and the separate performances of which are 'scored' in three large drawing-books, a pale shadow of the eighty minutes of strange, somnambulistic action which took place at the time. Here Fugard attempted an apparently total reliance upon the 'creative' as opposed to merely 'illustrative' abilities of his cast, two women and a man. Yet the 'truth' discovered was the result of the performers responding to the director–scribe's challenges, expressed as a complex of images Fugard derived from ancient and modern sources; the playwright himself remained in charge. This 'new' type of theatre focused on an event very close to South Africans – and, especially, white liberals: the explosion of a bomb as an act of protest on Johannesburg station, which killed an elderly white woman and led to the execution of its perpetrator, a white schoolteacher. If *Orestes* represents an extreme, even a limit, to what Fugard has been able to do in the theatre, this may have more to do with its subject, than with what ideas about the theatre released in him. The play explored the effect of violence upon those who carry it out: the central image was created by the slow, deliberate and silent destruction in each performance of a unique, irreplaceable and innocent object – a chair – by the actress, who sank down eventually into the debris, exhausted and terrified by what she had done. In a context in which violence is breeding more violence, this image is important; but, if Fugard persistently condemns violence, he is also careful to show its inevitability in a society which has adopted violent means to stifle opposition and prevent change.

His position is one that deserves respect; but not adulation. To understand it, it is necessary to have at least a minimal grasp of his situation, and the situation in which his plays occur. All his works reveal life under the system of racial legislation operating in South Africa since just after

13

the Second World War and known as apartheid or 'separate development' – two definitions of the same thing,
summing up its (to its critics) 'negative' aspects and (to its
supporters) 'positive' aspects. Many of the typical features
of apartheid existed before and during the war, but it was
the election victory of the Afrikaner Nationalist Party in
1948 which led to the creation of a system, and an ideology,
of segregation. Legislation was soon passed to prohibit
'mixed' marriages and sex across colour lines; a population
register was created, in which everyone was classified
according to race; a Group Areas Act (1950) enforced
residential segregation in towns and between all races; and
there was an increased insistence on 'social' or 'petty'
apartheid – that is, segregation in public places (including
theatres and cinemas), in the use of public transport, lifts
and lavatories. The longstanding laws reserving skilled jobs
for whites and preventing black workers from combining to
demand improvements in wages or conditions were tightened up. The promised 'positive' side was slow to appear –
indeed, it can hardly be discerned yet. Certain parts of the
country (amounting to some 13 per cent of the land area)
had long been 'reserved' for African occupation; these
were to become black 'homelands' or, as they are now
called, 'Bantustans'. Here blacks are supposed to enjoy
'separate but equal' rights so that there is no injustice in
their dispossession of such rights in the white areas. Here
they are obliged to go when the white economy has no need
of them, returning to the 'traditional' role of peasant or
small farmer, ruled by 'traditional' (government-
appointed) chiefs. In recent years there has been some
easing of 'petty' apartheid, and in the laws governing
trade-union activity. A new 'consultative' structure (involving the 'Coloured' and Asian minorities) is being introduced. But the basic power structure of the country, with

the whites controlling and exploiting the blacks, remains unaltered. The very existence of a place such as Soweto, its name derived from the soulless official title 'South-Western Townships', makes nonsense of the apartheid or separate-development theory: originally a 'temporary' slum-clearance scheme on the outskirts of Johannesburg, it is now a vast, sprawling ghetto city of nearly 2 million people, all black, who 'service' the white city, its mines, industries, transport and homes, and without whom Johannesburg would collapse overnight. And yet these people are supposed to be temporary sojourners, and given fewer rights than if they were. All 'white' South African cities have their equivalent supporting satellites, containing the largest concentration of urbanised proletariat on the African continent.

Such a scandalous system has, of course, provoked opposition and resistance. Until the early sixties, the black political response was generally conciliatory, the overall aim of successive organisations being to bring the white rulers to the negotiating table for a just dispensation in a shared society. Fugard's home ground, the Eastern Cape, has from the beginning been the nursery of black political leaders, mainly because it was the home of black education in South Africa. The three most important black leaders in recent years have all been Eastern Cape men – Nelson Mandela, Robert Sobukwe and Steve Biko. Only Mandela still lives, the imprisoned hero of the black masses, continuing leader of the ANC (African National Congress, founded 1912). Many thinking whites have recognised and admitted the contradictions and injustices of the apartheid system, including, most notably, the 'liberals'. Fugard may be said to belong to the 'liberals', who represent an attitude rather than a party.

It may seem too easy simply to label him 'liberal' or,

more broadly, 'liberal humanist'. But he has acknowledged that, if 'the old Liberal Party of South Africa still existed, I'd feel obliged to identify with it'.[8] The 'old Liberal Party' was founded in 1953 in response to the 1948 election result and the manifest inadequacy of the opposition United Party to resist the implementation of apartheid. It was disbanded in 1968, when multiracial political parties became illegal. The one absolute in the liberal viewpoint as it is expressed through such bodies as the English churches and the South African Institute of Race Relations, as well as by a wide range of prominent individuals not necessarily connected with the current legal survivor, the Progressive Federal Party, consists in the value and dignity of the individual. This is reflected in a tradition of deep human concern, and resistance towards totalitarian and nationalist views; equally it is reflected in a naïve faith in the reforming potential of personal moral pressure, associated with a failure to recognise the real centres of power. South African liberals tend to come from the intelligentsia: university lecturers and students, lawyers, clergymen, schoolteachers, journalists – and writers. Alan Paton was first vice-president of the 'old Liberal Party', and its leader when the decision was taken to disband. The Liberal Party was disproportionately white, but at least only some 40 per cent belonged to the dominant race, and Indians were also overrepresented. The vast bulk were English-speaking, although some Afrikaner intellectuals also belonged. Liberals want to 'build bridges', to 'enter into a dialogue', phrases which continue to be used by well-meaning individuals such as Fugard, but with less and less conviction. For, as Pierre van den Berghe has said,

> The madness inherent in apartheid leaves no room for compromise or adaptation. Apartheid can only be bols-

tered by coercion and violence, else it must collapse utterly. . . . To nearly all whites, the benefits of apartheid greatly overshadow the marginal inconveniences (such as military service). Only open, large-scale insurrection by blacks will alter the cost–benefit ratio for whites.[9]

The stumbling-block for liberals has always been their commitment to constitutional and parliamentary means, while the mass of the people are ruled by a tiny minority entrenched by law. As some liberals have become more sympathetic towards extra-parliamentary strategies such as passive resistance, boycotts and strikes – adopted perforce by the black opposition movements – government action has ensured their identification and silencing by imprisonment, banning or exile.

Fugard has survived all this, while continuing to express 'liberal' views. The South African experience which emerges in his plays is bitter and painful to contemplate; but, at the same time, there is a deep faith in the potential for survival of the individual human being. He wants to 'bear witness' to what is happening in his time. This is another way of saying that, as he puts it,

as a South African I want to talk to other South Africans about what is happening here and now. Now, being a South African means that I have got to acknowledge the fact that my whole style of living, everything, comes down to . . . how many decisions have I got that are not related to my white skin? I can only acknowledge that these exist, that they are facts. . . . Thorn trees don't protest the endless drought of the Karroo. . . . They just go on trying to grow. Just a basic survival informs the final, mutilated, stunted protest. . . .[10]

Fugard's plays are all, on some level, more or less explicitly, a protest about the quality of life in South Africa. To ignore this would be to render them meaningless. Many critics (especially in South Africa) prefer to stress their 'universi-tality'; and so help maintain the status quo. He himself prefers not to be called a 'political playwright'; nor am I suggesting that he is; but, in embodying what he sees as the 'truth' of his place in his work, in his textures and imagery, he cannot help but also embody its politics. Failure to recognise or admit this involves a failure to respond to his kind of theatre, as well as to what he is saying.

2
Career and Personal Influences

Harold Athol Lannigan Fugard was born on 11 June 1932, on a farm near Middelburg, Cape Province – a dry, dusty little village in the semi-desert Karroo region of South Africa. His parents ran a small general dealer's 'cash store' in Middelburg. His father, Harold, a crippled former jazz pianist was descended from Manchester immigrants, possibly Irish Catholic in origin, 'sort of good, English-speaking Eastern Cape stock'. His mother, Elizabeth Magdalena, *née* Potgieter, carried the name of one of the foremost Voortrekker families, long settled in the Karroo. Fugard's parents came from different worlds, yet, 'because of the strength of my mother's personality the Afrikaner culture was more dominant'.[1]

Fugard was, as he puts it, of 'mixed descent' in white South African terms.[2] He has inherited both the Afrikaans-speaking, narrowly Calvinist but independent attitudes of his mother's background; and the English-speaking, broadly Christian, more liberal-minded and outward-looking attitudes of his father's. But, if his mother's influence is felt to be ultimately the stronger, he was educated in English, and chose to write in English. Many of the characters in his plays would naturally speak Afrikaans; and what he calls their 'textures' or moods are derived from the Cape Afrikaner culture. But Fugard 'translates' them (his phrase) into English – or, more accurately, into his uniquely South African idiom, mixing English, Afrikaans and, sometimes, African speech in a way which enables him to be understood by a world audience without sacrificing too much of his local 'specifics'. Only H. C. Bosman (1905–51), the brilliant Afrikaner short-story writer who also adopted English as his medium, has approached Fugard's achievement in this respect.

In 1935 the family moved to Port Elizabeth, where they lived to begin with in a boarding-house run by Mrs Fugard. Port Elizabeth has been Fugard's home ever since. Short spells in larger centres such as Cape Town, Johannesburg or abroad have made no difference: 'I cannot conceive of myself as separate from it.'[3] It is the setting for most of his best work, with the exception of *The Island*, although the prisoners in that play do come from New Brighton, Port Elizabeth. Fugard always returns to Port Elizabeth, literally and metaphorically. If he often feels it is painful to continue living there, he also, apparently, feels unable to function anywhere else. He has 'acquired the code' there, that 'degree of familiarity which is necessary for me. . . . I must know exactly the textures that I'm going to deal with. I need that confidence before I can even start writing. . . .'[4]

In 1938 Fugard entered the Catholic Marist Brothers College in Port Elizabeth. While his mother continued to keep the family, 'Hally' (as he was called until his teens) began his secondary education on a council scholarship at the local technical college, where he had his first experience of amateur dramatics, both as an actor and as director of the school play. A course in motor mechanics reflected his interest in cars, an interest in which re-emerges in the fantasy sequence in *The Blood Knot* and in the TV play *Mille Miglia* (1968). Like many a poorly educated author before him, the teenage Fugard was reading (in Dickens's phrase) 'as if for life'; he had begun writing too.

A scholarship took Fugard to the University of Cape Town, one of the 'liberal', English-language universities of South Africa, where he was influenced by the remarkable Catholic existentialist Professor of Ethics, Martin Versfeld. The notion of dialogue is central to Versfeld: how it might be possible to communicate with, indeed love, one another, without exploitation. Like Fugard, he is obsessed with the possibility of love in a hate-ridden country. Unlike Fugard, Versfeld is a deeply committed Christian.

Fugard's lifelong interest in Camus began at this time, as did his interest in the evolutionary theories of Darwin and T. H. Huxley (explicit in *Statements after an Arrest*). If the subjects of study were important to him at Cape Town, gaining a degree was not – or so he decided two months before his finals when, in 1953, with Perseus Adams, a fellow student who was to become a poet, he set off to hitch-hike up Africa with £60 and ten tins of sardines. After crossing the Congo and Tanganyika (Tanzania), they reached Juba, Sudan, where they separated, and Fugard signed on as a deckhand on the British trampsteamer *SS Graigaur*, at a shilling a day. From the Malacca Straits he wrote to his mother, 'I am busy on the completion of the novel started in Cape Town. . . . I am deeply satisfied with my writing; there exists no doubt now in my mind that it is the one thing I have always been destined to do.'[5] He threw the novel (his second attempt) away. Within a year he was back home, working as a freelance journalist for the Port Elizabeth *Evening Post*. He now knew what he wanted to do, but had yet to find the right medium.

Fugard has often said that the ten-month experience of living and working side-by-side with men of all races on the *Graigaur* liberated him from the prejudice endemic among those with his background. Nadine Gordimer claims that every white South African needs to be born twice: the second time into an awareness of racialism. But, unlike other white South African liberal writers, such as Gordimer (or Alan Paton or Dan Jacobson), for Fugard this has meant turning against his own people, becoming a traitor to his mother's, if not his father's, race. This helps explain the painful, guilt-ridden intensity with which the racial issue is treated in most of his plays; and his reiterated assertion that he is an Afrikaner, with no other home than South Africa. He tends to ignore the English side of his background and upbringing, and subscribes to the myth that English-speaking white South Africans find it easier or more profitable to leave the country than Afrikaners.

Fugard has traced his sense of guilt and remorse over what happens to black people to a specific incident in his Port Elizabeth childhood: 'I spat in the face of a black man. I cannot talk about it to this day. I bear the guilt.' He calls himself the 'classic example of the impotent white liberal'.[6] Yet such feelings provide the impetus for his plays. And that painful childhood incident has finally found a place in *'Master Harold' . . . and the boys*. The black man involved was Sam Semela, a Basuto waiter in the Fugard boarding-house who went on to work for the family for some fifteen years. Fugard remembers him as the 'most significant – the only – friend' of his boyhood years. When he was about thirteen, and helping behind the counter in the St George's

Park tearoom while Semela waited at table, he and the man had 'a rare quarrel', the subject of which is now forgotten.

> In a truculent silence we closed the café, Sam set off home to New Brighton on foot and I followed a few minutes later on my bike. I saw him walking ahead of me and, coming out of a spasm of acute loneliness, as I rode behind him I called his name, he turned in mid-stride to look back and, as I cycled past, I spat in his face. Don't suppose I will ever deal with the shame that overwhelmed me the second after I had done that.[7]

Fugard was first inspired to become actively involved in drama when he met his wife, Sheila Meiring, at the time an actress in Cape Town. Like Fugard, Sheila Meiring was half-Afrikaner, half-English; she is now a prominent South African novelist and poet, who writes in English. Fugard had obtained a post writing news bulletins for the South African Broadcasting Corporation in Cape Town, and was writing short stories in his spare time; but after his marriage to Sheila in September 1956 the theatre became his goal. A last-minute walk-on part in a production in which Sheila was playing (and Yvonne Bryceland was in the lead) was followed by the role of the messenger in an acclaimed version of *Oedipus Rex*. Thereafter the two formed a theatre workshop called Circle Players – all amateurs, who hired the Labia Theatre in Cape Town for Sunday night performances after which a collection was taken to cover costs. Sheila directed and did most of the writing; her husband acted, then began to contribute 'some rather pretentious little pieces', including a lost verse-drama, *The Cell*, under the influence of J. M. Synge.[8] Like other writers to whom he was attracted at the time, such as William

Faulkner and Tennessee Williams, the main significance of Synge's work was that it confirmed the growing sense that he wanted to write drama that was, above all, local.

But it was not until 1958, when the Fugards moved to Johannesburg, attracted by the possibility of work in South Africa's largest city, that this instinct began to find its true inspiration. The Fugards were introduced to Sophiatown, the multiracial ghetto full of violence, energy and talent, by Benjamin Pogrund, a liberal journalist friend from Cape Town. The only job Fugard could find at first was as clerk in a 'Native Commissioner's Court' where pass-law offenders were tried. It was an important experience for him. He knew his society was evil before then, 'but seeing the machinery in operation taught me how it works and in fact what it does to people'. Few white South Africans have seen or are aware of what happens in such places. 'I think my basic pessimism was born there, watching that procession of faces and being unable to relate to them.'[9] But, at the same time, Fugard made his first black friends in the 'township'; and out of their lives he created *No-Good Friday* and *Nongogo*, both written for and performed by black amateur casts. The key to life in the townships was (and is) *survival*; this became a central theme in his work. The Fugards created an African Theatre Workshop, using Method techniques and drawing on the talents of a remarkable group of people, including Lewis Nkosi, Bloke Modisane, Can Themba, Nat Nakasa, and one splendid actor – Zakes Mokae, for whom he was to write the part of Zach in *The Blood Knot*.

The idea for *The Blood Knot* came to Fugard in London in 1960. The small local success of the Sophiatown plays had enabled him – with the help of a visiting Belgian director, Tone Brulin – to obtain his first work in the professional theatre, as stage manager with the (all-white)

National Theatre Organisation of South Africa (founded in 1947 to promote drama in English and Afrikaans, dissolved fifteen years later into four separate provincial Performing Arts Councils). In a few months, Fugard worked on plays by Shaw, Beckett, Ionesco, Pirandello, the South African James Ambrose Brown, and others. It was, he recalled later, a 'crash course' in modern drama; and it whetted his appetite for further professional experience. Soon he and Sheila had saved enough to leave for Europe, like many aspiring young colonials before and since.

In London in the autumn of 1959, they resorted to odd jobs to keep going, and pay for theatre tickets. Tone Brulin, back in Belgium, invited them over to help form the New Africa Group with South African David Herbert; and, in May 1960 the group successfully presented Herbert's 'try for white' play (i.e. a play about a black passing for a white), *A Kakamas Greek*, with Fugard in the title role, at a Festival of Avant-Garde Theatre in Brussels. Some touring followed, but by the end of the year, with Sheila pregnant and no further work in prospect, the Fugards had returned home to Port Elizabeth, where *The Blood Knot* was completed.

Barney Simon, a year younger than Fugard and from a similarly near-poor-white background, had met the playwright briefly in 1959 just before the Fugards left for Europe; he had himself already visited London, where he had worked with Joan Littlewood and developed a strong passion for the small-scale, 'workshop' ventures she initiated; he was the only talent in white South African theatre to provide Fugard with any significant stimulation as a writer and director. His help in being the 'third eye' on *The Blood Knot* was invaluable. In March 1962 the final (140th) performance of the play took place in New Brighton, Port Elizabeth. The following year it was launched at the New Arts Theatre, Hampstead, London, with Zakes Mokae and Ian Bannen, directed by John Berry. In 1964 Berry directed it at the Cricket Theatre, New York, with James Earl Jones and J. D. Cannon. The *New York Times* voted it the best play of the year. Fugard's international career had begun.

The Blood Knot established the essentials of Fugard drama; and during the following years Fugard wrote three more plays along the same lines: *Hello and Goodbye*, which was first directed by Barney Simon, with Fugard as Johnnie and Molly Seftel as Hester, in the Library Theatre, Johannesburg, after 'previews' in Dorkay House; *People Are Living There*, which, after failing to find a local sponsor, opened at the Close Theatre, Glasgow, in March 1968, directed by Robin Midgley, who had impressed Fugard with his direction of *The Blood Knot* for BBC TV the previous year; and *Boesman and Lena*, an early version of which opened in the Rhodes University Little Theatre, Grahamstown, on 10 July 1969, directed by Fugard, with himself as Boesman and Yvonne Bryceland as Lena. Earlier that year Yvonne Bryceland, one of South Africa's most experienced professional actresses, had been cast as Milly for what became a much-acclaimed production, mounted by the Cape Performing Arts Board, of *People Are Living There*; Barney Simon and actor–impresario Percy Sieff had been pressing Fugard to consider her for a role, and suddenly the playwright realised he had found another person whose creative acting-potential was to prove an essential resource.

Fugard's passport was taken away in 1967, 'for reasons of state safety and security', the day after a performance of *The Blood Knot* on British television. He did not cease work; nor leave the country on a one-way 'exit permit', which is what he felt the authorities were after. Instead, he continued to write, direct and perform; and to speak out against what he saw was wrong. He had initiated an international playwrights' boycott of South Africa in 1963, to provoke a response from local theatre managements who had accepted segregated audiences before being forced to do so by law; but when such legislation was introduced he reversed his tactics on the ground, he said, that keeping South Africans isolated from the ideas of the 'free West' was just what the government wanted. More recently, theatres have once again been desegregated, in the sense that audiences and casts may be 'mixed' if a suitable permit is applied for. Any theatre which does so apply, however, may find itself boycotted by blacks who consider that such applications represent an acceptance of 'the system'. Fugard, most of whose plays in any case first appear in 'unofficial' fringe venues, continues to allow his plays to be produced as long as 'all races' may see them.

In 1971, after a public petition helped secure the passport which had been withdrawn in 1967, Fugard accepted an invitation from Nicholas Wright to direct *Boesman and Lena* at the Royal Court Theatre Upstairs, with Bryceland as Lena, Mokae as Boesman and Bloke Modisane as Outa. The production was an immediate success, and transferred to the Young Vic. The interest of Ross Devenish, a young South African freelance television documentary film-maker, was aroused, and he persuaded Fugard to collaborate on a film version, with Fugard himself and Bryceland in the title roles. The success of *Boesman and Lena* at the Edinburgh and London Film Festivals in the autumn of 1973 led to further work together, and the televising of other Fugard plays in South Africa. Devenish directed *The Guest at Steenkampskraal*, Fugard's account of an episode in the life of the tormented Afrikaans poet and amateur zoologist Eugène Marais

(1871–1936), premiered on BBC2 TV on 5 March 1977, with Fugard in the main role; and in 1979 Devenish and Fugard made the film *Marigolds in August* on location near Port Elizabeth, with John Kani and Winston Ntshona. Film-making is 'not remotely as meaningful' as theatre for Fugard.[10] But the collaboration with Devenish at least involved some success in reaching a new, larger audience, as well as experiment in a new medium.

The response of the Royal Court – in particular that of its moving spirit, Oscar Lewenstein – was of great importance to Fugard. The freedom and commitment which characterised the English Stage Company had made the Court a desirable place in which to work from the time of Fugard's earlier London visit. By the mid seventies, as a result of Lewenstein's faith in his potential, the Court was offering the public a 'South African Season', including the three *Statements* plays, which became the foundation of Fugard's reputation abroad, as well as that of his co-creators and actors, Yvonne Bryceland, John Kani and Winston Ntshona. Fugard later observed that 'there was an area of trust' at the Court that was 'very special, a space that allowed me to make mistakes'.[11]

It was something he had long yearned to have in South Africa. Back home after the first overseas production of *Boesman and Lena* in 1971, Fugard had begun discussions with Yvonne Bryceland's husband, the Cape Town photographer Brian Astbury, on forming an experimental theatre and obtaining a site at which to perform new plays. By March 1972, after some hectic months, a new chapter in the history of South African theatre began with the opening in a converted warehouse near the old Malay quarter of Cape Town of the Space/die Ruimte/Indawo – its English name derived from the Open Space in Tottenham Court Road, as well as from Peter Brook's seminal book, *The*

Empty Space (1968). Under Astbury's courageous if erratic management (it was his first experience with theatre), the Space became the venue for all that was exciting in South African theatre outside the black 'townships' for the next seven years. Sometimes it also played host to the best of 'township' drama, such as the remarkable *Imfuduso*, created by the women of Crossroads, the infamous squatter camp on the outskirts of Cape Town.

Fugard's work was essential to the success of the Space. An early version of *Statements after an Arrest*, with Fugard and Bryceland in the leading roles, was commissioned as the opening production; it was succeeded by *Sizwe Banzi Is Dead* (original spelling), with a facsimile passbook as programme; the following year (1973) *Die Hodoshe Span*, the first version of *The Island*, was conceived and rehearsed at the Space, while Fugard, Kani and Ntshona awaited passports for the *Sizwe Bansi* tour of Britain. Miraculously, the Space evaded theatre segregation laws as well as censorship – although not without some close brushes with the authorities.

Fugard's career is marked by attempts to create a suitable 'space' for a specifically African theatre: first there was the African Theatre Workshop in Sophiatown in 1958–9; then the New Africa Group in Brussels in 1960; an ill-advised visit to Lusaka in 1964 to direct *The Caucasian Chalk Circle*, which had to be abandoned as a result of conflict with the Zambian authorities over alleged 'discrimination'; the Ijinle Company at the Hampstead Theatre Club, with Zakes Mokae and others, supposed to become a base for African theatre in London, but which folded after a production of Wole Soyinka's *The Trials of Brother Jero* in 1966; and the Space in Cape Town, which staggered on for years, despite the departure of Astbury and Bryceland for London, and its removal to new premises, but which has now finally closed; and, most recently, the Market Theatre in Johannesburg, created not by Fugard but by Barney Simon and others in an old fruit market, a site excluded from the Group Areas Act, which has successfully evaded theatre segregation and proved an essential venue for Fugard, whose *A Lesson from Aloes* was premiered there in 1978, and where '*Master Harold*' *. . and the boys* had its local premiere in 1983.

What is missing from all these ventures is any significant initiative from black people. They represent well-intentioned 'liberal' bridge-building efforts. This is evident from the single most successful involvement of a white playwright and director in black theatre: Fugard and the Serpent Players. After seeing *The Blood Knot* in New Brighton, and hearing of Fugard's Sophiatown workshop, a group of men from the Port Elizabeth township of New Brighton approached the playwright at his home in Port Elizabeth in 1963: Norman Ntshinga, Welcome Duru, Fats Bokhilane and Mike Ngxcolo. Only the involvement of talented and committed whites such as Fugard could provide access to the craft, experience and facilities they desired. Within two years of that initial approach, the group known as the Serpent Players had worked on five productions under Fugard's enthusiastic direction, rehearsing where they could on budgets of around £20 per production. Fugard was helping to satisfy the hunger to articulate their experiences evident in the lives of ordinary black people. But, on the day when a local adaptation of *The Caucasian Chalk Circle* by the Serpent Players was due to open, the leading actor was arrested; a purge of the township had begun. A number of the Players were arrested, tried, and imprisoned on Robben Island. Out of these events grew the making of plays without an identifiable author, improvisation, and new experiments with the creative potential of the actors – especially, with two remarkably gifted men who joined the Serpent Players in 1965 (John Kani) and 1967 (Winston Ntshona). *The Coat* was performed as an 'acting-exercise' before a white 'theatre appreciation' group in Port Elizabeth in 1966, and was followed by many similar experiments, the most important of which turned out to be *Sizwe Bansi Is Dead* and *The Island*. The acclaim abroad for these two works enabled Kani and Ntshona to become successful performers in their own right, but it took them away from the Serpent Players – which, with its members in prison or robbed of initiative by police harassment, now languishes.

After the success of the *Statements* plays during the early seventies, a note of exhaustion appears in Fugard. While events in South Africa were building up to the riots of June 1976, the playwright was turning inwards, towards more personal, abstract concerns – evident in the relatively ineffective *Dimetos*, commissioned for the Edinburgh Festival in 1975, and revised the following year for a no more successful production with Paul Scofield in the title role. After more than ten years in their small bungalow at Schoenmaker's Kop, a village perched upon a headland some miles along the coast from Port Elizabeth, the Fugards retreated to a new home they built for themselves near Sardinia Bay, 'The Ashram' – a name reflecting Sheila Fugard's conversion to Buddhism.

Here Fugard awaits further inspiration – what he calls new 'appointments'. That he does not wait in vain is testified by the success of '*Master Harold*' . . . *and the boys*, premiered on 10 March 1982 at the Yale Repertory Theatre and directed by the playwright himself. This is his most personal play, and travels furthest back into his own past. It has been remarkably successful in America, South

Africa and Britain. Appropriately, the original cast of three included an actor first met in Sophiatown, and now living in New York – Zakes Mokae.

3
The Sophiatown Plays

Athol Fugard's first real 'appointment' as a playwright was with Sophiatown. Out of his encounter with this remarkable, long-since demolished town within a town and its people grew his first two full-length plays, *No-Good Friday* and *Nongogo*. Although, as Fugard himself willing admits, the plays now look like rather naïve apprenticeship work, they remain unique examples of an attempt by a white South African writer to enter into and understand the day-to-day sufferings of his black countrymen. Both plays were created in drama workshops conducted with amateurs from the 'township', and were first performed in rough, makeshift conditions. They are somewhat derivative, contrived and melodramatic works; yet they both continue to exert a certain power, and are, on occasion, successfully revived – as they were, for example, by Temba Theatre Company at the Crucible Theatre, Sheffield, in 1974.

No-Good Friday and *Nongogo* are largely naturalistic in manner; and their main impact is correspondingly as a reflection of the experiences of the township characters –

jazz musician, gangster, aspiring correspondence student, 'shebeen queen', door-to-door salesman – whose stories they tell. But, at a deeper level, they also go some way towards suggesting the fundamental corruption and exploitation of black people in South African society. This was probably not a part of Fugard's conscious purpose. What interested him most was what becomes a familiar, lasting theme in his work: the cost of survival under extreme conditions.

No-Good Friday is about Willie Seopola, the self-taught township intellectual who decides to make a stand against Shark, the protection racketeer who collects his 'insurance' on Fridays. As the unemployed saxophone-player Guy tells Father Higgins (the only white role in these two plays), 'You can forget about the police. They protect a fellow like Shark. You see they're only interested in our passes. But a Kaffir laying a charge against a criminal . . . that would be a joke.' Willie implicitly questions both this assumption and the system which has created it, by his action in reporting the gangster's murder of a non-compliant and uncomprehending rural newcomer, Tobias; his own murder follows inevitably, although the play ends before we see it.

Nongogo is about a shebeen proprietress, Queeny, who tries to escape her past as a mineworkers' whore (a 'Nongogo', or a woman for 2s 6d) and lead a 'respectable' life; and her encounter with Johnny, the aspiring township tablecloth-salesman trying to forget his humiliation at having been raped in the mineworkers' compound. Neither play offers much hope. Both make it very clear that being black in South Africa is not a situation in which hope comes easily. Yet Fugard, as a white liberal, wishes to believe in the possibility of individual action, even if what he himself saw and experienced in Sophiatown contradicts this possibility. The contradiction is rooted deeply in the history and politics of the period, which it is only possible to suggest briefly here.

For the first ten years after their electoral success in 1948, the Nationalist Party ruled to an accompaniment of almost continual protest and disturbance; contact between radicals of all races encouraged the belief that co-operation in the fight against discrimination was possible and necessary. But, already in 1950, widespread rioting on the Rand, although clearly (according to a commission of inquiry) the result of resentment at the pass laws, liquor raids and inadequate amenities generally in the townships, had led to the Suppression of Communism Act – the first and most important of an unending series of legislative attempts to stifle opposition to apartheid. The Communist Party was declared unlawful, its members banned without appeal; and the definition of 'Communist' was expanded to include anyone promoting social or political change by 'unlawful' means, or by encouraging 'hostility' between the races.

In 1952, the 300th anniversary of the founding by the Dutch of a 'refreshment station' at the Cape, a Defiance Campaign was launched, during which some 8000 people were imprisoned for voluntarily contravening apartheid regulations – to no avail. Chief Albert Luthuli, a deeply committed Christian and leader of the ANC, was banned. In June 1955, 3000 delegates of all races adopted a Freedom Charter based on the United Nations Declaration of Human Rights. But the bannings and penalties for opposition increased until, towards the end of the following year, 156 people were arrested in a massive raid, to stand trial under the Suppression of Communism Act and for high treason. Religious and other bodies in South Africa and abroad provided legal and financial aid; and after four years all the accused in the Treason Trial (as it became known) had had their charges dropped or were found not guilty. But by then the Sharpeville massacre had taken place, and a new era of repression begun.

Benjamin Pogrund, the liberal journalist who advised the eager but inexperienced Fugards to leave Cape Town for Johannesburg, was one of those who believed in crossing racial barriers. He recommended Fugard to his friends in Sophiatown, the 'lusty, slummy township' it was still just possible for whites to enter freely (permits are required for any designated black area). Sophiatown was 'the most lively, important and sophisticated' of all the African townships; in its 'crowded and narrow streets walked philosophers and gangsters, musicians and pick-pockets, short-story writers and businessmen'; it 'embodied all that was best and worst of African life in towns'.[1] Unlike other townships, it had grown up as part of the 'white' city. 'White' liquor was not available to blacks by law, and so organised crime stepped in: whites bought liquor in bulk and resold it at vast profit to black bootleg-gers and shebeen queens, who in turn required protection outside the law, which they obtained from black mobsters such as the notorious 'Boy' Faraday (Queeny in *Nongogo* relies on her former pimp, Sam, and the ugly humpback Blackie). Running a shebeen or a gang represented a kind of success – a success magnified by the extent to which it involved bypassing the white system of control over black lives.

By the time the Fugards arrived there in 1958, Sophiatown had already been rezoned for whites only under an extension of the Group Areas Act and renamed Triomf (Afrikaans for 'triumph'), although the massive removal scheme, conducted against a continuous chorus of protest, was still far from complete. Fugard's first job, as clerk of the 'Native Commissioner's Court' in Fordsburg, where he watched the daily procession of pass-law cases, forced him to understand the basis of his countrymen's suffering. At the same time, his new friends in Sophiatown offered, as he put it, 'the most stimulating and promising field for a young playwright . . . tremendous poverty, a capacity for humour that is almost proverbial, bitterness and hope'.[2] Above all, the ability to survive. These qualities he tried to express in the Sophiatown plays.

No-Good Friday opens in a 'typical' Sophiatown back-yard, late one Friday afternoon. A young woman is busy taking down tattered clothes from a washing-line strung between rusting sheets of corrugated iron. Sounds off indicate the domestic bustle of others preparing for the return of wage-earners with their pay packets – or tales of woe, such as that recounted by Guy, the saxophonist, whose entry initiates the action. Guy tells Rebecca of his futile search for employment in 'Goli' (the city of gold, i.e. Johannesburg). As their conversation shifts to Rebecca's man Willie, the main character and theme of the play are introduced: Willie is in his 'First year BA Correspondent'; it is his aim thereby to become 'independent'. 'A big word, isn't it?' remarks Rebecca, an edge of bitterness in her voice. 'He just doesn't need anyone.' But, counters Guy, 'you can't always add up on paper what a man needs, like your instalments on the stove each month'.

The homely, proverbial image reinforces the main point: Willie's needs will turn out to be more demanding than any of them, including Willie himself, could anticipate. Rebecca exits into the shack. The shack's interior will provide the setting for Scenes iii and iv, in effect framed by the exterior, backyard scenes which make the rest of this five-scene play. Fugard thus ensures that, structurally and visually, the private, 'interior' world Rebecca wishes to preserve, as she wishes to preserve her relationship with Willie, is dominated by their environment, the 'outside' world of township life which ultimately destroys her hopes.

Before Willie himself enters, Fugard exposes another typical element of township life: Watson, the 'politician', whose 'work' for the day has consisted of thinking up ideas for the 'delegates' at that night's meeting. Guy accuses him, 'You don't walk the streets looking for a job like me.' Watson replies, 'You too must make sacrifices for the cause, otherwise the heavy boot of oppression will for ever be on our backs! Hey, that's good. (*He makes a note*.)' Of course, we laugh. But the laugh is too easily come by. As Robert MacLaren has pointed out, although there were undoubtedly politicians such as this at the time (there always are), without any other representative of political organisations in these plays, or any other indication of black political awareness, the effect is to discredit political action and distort the legitimate and pressing political needs to which Watson's rhetoric refers.[3] The possibility of *joint* action against the gangsters or the white authorities, or both, is not imagined; and so Willie's stand against Shark must inevitably be his alone, the single individual who, almost miraculously, resists the compromise which corrupts all the others.

It is the fate of the peasant Tobias that provokes Willie's lone rebellion. Guy plays 'Friday Night Blues' (a motif which will also conclude the play) to mark Willie's entrance; and when he plays it again Tobias, the 'Blanketboy' from the rural 'reserves', arrives, brought in by the sympathetic white missionary, Father Higgins. Tobias's nickname identifies what distinguishes him most obviously from the others on stage: his rural 'uniform', the characteristic, brightly coloured blanket. Willie, Guy and the others are dressed in American-style clothes, second-hand or cast-offs. As the pathetic, dazed figure arrives, he provokes Willie to a bitter outburst:

WILLIE. Why do they do it?
HIGGINS. Do what?
WILLIE. That! Why do they come here, like *that*!
HIGGINS. He only wants to live, Willie. . . .

The moment is visually arresting, a gesture, an image which resonates through the play. If any single moment* in *No-Good Friday* can be said to sum up dramatically what it is about, it is this one. Significantly, the image reappears, fourteen years later, in *Sizwe Bansi Is Dead*, when the shy, uncertain and unsophisticated Robert Zwelinzima arrives at Styles's studio for the 'snap' he wishes to send back to his wife in the Ciskei Bantustan.

It is an image both potent and familiar: there stands the innocent peasant or farmworker, drawn to the city by forces he is unable to resist or understand. The specifically South African aspect of this image derives from a fact central to the apartheid system: such peasants are 'surplus' labour, left or dumped in the 'reserves' (now Bantustans) until 'required' by the white economy. Of course, since there is very little work in the undeveloped reserves, men such as Tobias or Robert Zwelinzima are bound to leave for the urban areas, despite the laws created to control their movements. That Fugard does not deal with this subject unless provoked into doing so by the demands of the black people who become his actors suggests how much more important it is to them than to him; it also suggests why his depiction of Tobias is severely limited, even sentimental. The potential for sentimentality is, of course, always there: identifying with someone else's problems carries this danger with it, and Fugard does not wholly escape. He is unable to identify fully with the complexity of the problem. In the letter Tobias composes aloud – a letter to his wife, explaining what has happened to him ('Dear Maxulu', he

39

begins, 'I have arrived at Jo'burg. . . . They have buildings here like ten mission churches on top of one another, so high you cannot see the cross on top') – the author's hand is a little too obvious, as is the element of literary stereotyping. Tobias sounds like an earlier 'Jim come to Jo'burg' figure, the Reverend Kumalo in Alan Paton's *Cry the Beloved Country* (1948), who also speaks in the pseudo-biblical cadence of 'The grass is long, the oxen fat, the sun heavy' and so on.

But: 'Stop him dreaming' exclaims Willie. Tobias's presence constitutes a challenge precisely because he is a dreamer. Dreams are dangerous for the black man. The onward surge of the play towards the murder of Tobias at the end of Scene ii (for not complying with Shark's protection racket) is compelling; thereafter, the pace slackens, and the play loses itself in its concern for Willie's tortured conscience. The reason for this shift appears to be that, at least on one level, Willie functions as Fugard's alter ego: the self-made man out-of-key with his surroundings, the conscience of others. The only real survivor at the end of the play is Guy, the musician, who has found work with the white missionary, playing his sax for the mission show. Higgins, performed by 'Hal Lannigan' in the opening production – that is, by Fugard himself – thereby becomes the white man who helps black people express themselves, just as Fugard has done in putting on the play. *No-Good Friday* is thus curiously self-reflexive, reminding us of its author and his position, even as it offers us (mainly in the first half) the 'township' experience.

The essence of that experience is humiliation. This is evident first in Guy's attempts to get to work, then in the sadly humorous cameo of Pinkie, the 'tea-boy' who wants to know whether or not to apologise to his boss for something he has not done; but it is most powerfully expressed when Guy 'teaches' Tobias how the black man must behave towards the white in Johannesburg: 'yes *baas*, no *baas*, thank you *baas* . . . even when he kicks you up the backside'. It is a litany of servility, repeated word for word by Tobias in unconscious mockery. In his innocence, he goes on to mock Shark's authority too, later, when he laughs at the idea that he needs 'protection': 'I'm not a baby', he exclaims, sealing his own death warrant. His murder follows swiftly; it is the effective climax of the play.

The idea that humiliation and role-playing are essential for survival permeates Fugard's plays. In *Boesman and Lena* Boesman adopts the role Guy attempted to teach Tobias: he plays the servile underdog when the white man bulldozes his shack – '*Dankie, baas!*' A more fully developed version appears in *Sizwe Bansi*, when Buntu teaches Robert/Sizwe how to act the part of a man who has the correct pass. Such moments provide electrifying theatre, showing as they do that acting is 'for life', as well as a part of life. But in *No-Good Friday* it is not a means for effective survival, since Tobias is unable to learn it. The alternative, resistance, is equally futile, however, despite Fugard's attempt to suggest that

> The world I live in is the way it is not in spite of me but because of me. You think we're just poor suffering come-to-Jesus-at-the-end-of-it-all black men and that the world's all wrong and against us so what the hell. Well I'm not sure of that any more. I'm not so sure because I think we helped to make it, the way it is.

Yet Willie's subsequent action, reporting the murder of Tobias, and then passively waiting for Shark to take his revenge, hardly suggests an alternative to the black Christian martyrdom he so vehemently rejects. Fugard makes

41

him behave in the end as if he believes what he has rejected.

The confusion evident in *No-Good Friday* is apparent elsewhere in Fugard's work. *Tsotsi*, the novel he composed during and immediately after this period in Sophiatown (not published until twenty years later, in 1980), is about a brutal, unfeeling thug whose gang preys upon the innocent just as Shark's gang does in *No-Good Friday*. But the eponymous hero of *Tsotsi* is miraculously transformed by a nameless infant suddenly left in his care – a 'conversion' as improbable and stereotyped as in any minor Victorian novel or popular melodrama, which serves only to undercut the persuasive account of the appalling conditions in which he and his gang have come to live. The novel ends with its newly tender hero crushed to death while trying to save the child, beneath the wall of a Sophiatown house, bulldozed by the white authorities. Fugard cannot imagine a continuing life for his Tsotsi, despite the man's conversion. The gap between what seems possible for the black man in his world, and what Christianity holds out, seems unbridgeable. Increasingly, individual action becomes meaningless, an event leading nowhere. Not only does Christian hope disappear, but life seems to be pointless. Hence the tendency in Fugard's plays, from *The Blood Knot* onwards, for the plot or structure of action to become circular, directionless: providence is replaced by the absurd – a very painful transition for someone, such as Fugard, reared in the Calvinist tradition, but a transition enforced by what he observed of the pain and suffering in the townships.

No-Good Friday had its premiere on 30 August 1958 on the primitive 'stage' (proscenium arch and ordinary hall lighting) of the Bantu Men's Social Centre, where it nevertheless attracted sufficient attention to transfer subsequently for one, very important night at the Brooke Theatre in Johannesburg – an all-white venue in which

Lewis Nkosi substituted for Fugard as the white Father Higgins since a 'mixed' cast was forbidden. The 'critical European audience thundered with applause', according to *Zonk*, the popular African monthly, which praised Fugard for giving his unknown actors 'a wonderful vehicle in which they could show their talents', as well as revealing 'a great understanding of the African people and their way of life'.[4] The patronising tone is predictable, since the review was written by a white critic, who, however, did recognise the potential of its African cast – a potential almost completely stifled during the years which followed, as a result of bannings and exile.

Lewis Nkosi, who is now a well-known writer and critic in exile, was only one of the remarkable people with whom Fugard came into contact in Sophiatown in 1958–9. Before the removal of the 'township' by the government, an extraordinary flowering of black urban culture had occurred, which later writers such as Sipho Sepamla have labelled a 'Cultural Golden Age' – although, as Sepamla also points out, 'the very word "theatre" was not part of our vocabulary'.[5] It remained for whites such as Fugard to exploit the rich upsurge of talent before drama in the modern European sense could begin to emerge. There was a good deal of urban entertainment, performed in the few available school or church halls by such groups as the Manhattan Brothers or the Woody Woodpeckers, whose musical performances often included satirical, topical sketches. But inexperience and restrictions meant that black musicians and performers had to rely on white impresarios to manage and promote them, men such as Ike Brooks and Alfred Herbert (the latter's 'African Jazz and Variety Show' ran for fourteen years), who encouraged them to play in 'white' venues, since that was where the money was.

The climax of this form of cultural interaction came with the staging of *King Kong* by Union Artists in 1959. Based on the life of the African heavyweight boxer Ezekiel Dhlamini, with production, direction and script by whites, but using black singers, actors, musicians and a score by the 'township' composer Todd Matshikiza, *King Kong* attracted phenomenal local interest as well as, eventually, overseas contracts. It portrayed something of the frustrations and hardships of township life, while the music, in particular the voice of Miriam Makeba in the female lead, ten-year-old Lemmy Mambaso's penny-whistling, and the backing of the Jazz Dazzlers, gave something of the authentic township flavour – a brash and vibrant mixture of African, black American and European styles and contrasts. The success of *King Kong* led to a series of glossily packaged 'African' musicals and plays produced by whites with the blessing of the authorities, from *uMabatha* to *Ipi Tombi*, works which had less and less to do with township life, and more and more to do with offering white audiences at home and abroad an 'acceptable' image of the African.

Although Fugard's involvement in black-township life was part of a larger movement by well-meaning whites to take part in, if not exploit, the evident talents of black people, nothing could be further from the 'show' that *King Kong* and its successors offered than his own small, rough workshop ventures. *No-Good Friday* included a saxophone part for one of the actors, Cornelius ('Connie') Mabaso, who played Guy. But this was an earnest attempt to use the talent of a man who was subsequently to become a serious actor–playwright and so reflect the actual quality of life in Sophiatown, rather than the exploitation or 'packaging' of black experience which characterised later cultural interaction.

The 'Sophiatown group' which Fugard met, most of them

now dead or in exile, included 'one splendid actor in the person of Zakes Mokae'. Mokae struck Fugard as ideally suitable for a thug, a small role he gave him in *No-Good Friday*, in which he played one of Shark's murderous sidekicks. Fugard recalls a growing sense of Mokae 'being a very special person', which led him to write the role of Blackie, Queeny's crippled and violent hanger-on in *Nongogo*, especially for him, 'and this was the start of one of the really rich working relationships of my life – and also, of course, of a very important friendship'.[6] Fugard and Mokae met through the non-racial artists' equity organisation, the Union of South African Artists, in 1958. Mokae had never had an acting-lesson (not surprising in a country without drama schools for blacks), but he had had some minor film roles. Johannesburg-born and bred, he attended St Peter's Anglican school in Rosettenville, where he came to know Father Trevor Huddleston (whose *Naught for your Comfort* revealed the conditions in Sophiatown to the world). Huddleston, evidently the model for Father Higgins in *No-Good Friday*, formed a jazz band to which Mokae, an accomplished tenor saxophonist, belonged as a founder member. The unanticipated success of a farewell concert for the much-loved Anglican missionary, held in the Bantu Men's Social Centre in 1954 under the auspices of the Union of South African Artists, stimulated the growing interest in township culture; and Union Artists (as it became), under the leadership of theatrical promoter Ian Bernhardt, were able to acquire their own premises in Dorkay House, the factory warehouse where Bernhardt went on to present talent contests and minor jazz festivals for township performers, before mainly white audiences. The huge success of *King Kong* enabled Union Artists to begin a much-needed drama school and arts workshop – the African Music and Drama Association, which is still active – and to sponsor the Rehearsal Room, the private, experimental 'theatre' in which Fugard and Mokae first performed *The Blood Knot*.

But for *Nongogo* Fugard and his African cast had to make do with the Bantu Men's Social Centre and then Darrah Hall (a church basement), although these primitive conditions did enable him to introduce an innovation and stage the play 'in the round'. *Nongogo* is an altogether more carefully crafted and thought-out work than *No-Good Friday*, no doubt partly because by the time of writing it Fugard had obtained his first paid job in the theatre, as stage manager for the National Theatre Organisation, and through the NTO's experimental Kamertoneel (studio theatre) had come into contact with productions of modern European drama. But, despite this contact with 'official' mainstream theatre, Fugard continued to operate in the 'rough' and multiracial setting of Sophiatown. The way he operated is recalled by David Phetoe: 'A cousin of mine in 1959 was called in by Athol Fugard to do a part in a play called *Nongogo*. Fugard was still a rookie and crude and he walked into this building . . . with this *Nongogo*, about the life in Sophiatown, and my cousin was interested.' But the cousin soon realised that Phetoe himself would be better in the part, and told Fugard, who said, 'Tell your cousin to come in.'

> When I called Fugard he was already excited over the phone. He said, 'Your voice sounds very good. I'd like to see you.' I walked in here and I said, 'May I see Mr Fugard?.
>
> He said, 'Athol's my name.'
> I said, 'David Phetoe's mine.'
> 'Sit down. Have you done any plays before?'
> 'No.'

'Well can you read me a line or two?'

I just opened up the script and read and had hardly
finished one line when he said, 'Keep the script, it's
yours, and that's the character you'll be doing.' Just like
that. And I never stopped yet, in the theatre I mean.[7]

David Phetoe played Sam, Queeny's self-assured 'friend',
in the original production of *Nongogo*, Zakes Mokae
(Blackie) and Connie Mabaso (Patrick) maintained the
continuity of the workshop which had produced *No-Good
Friday*; while Tandi Khumalo as Queeny (suitably large
and blowzy) and Solomon Rashilo as Johnny completed the
cast.

The number of characters was halved for this, the second
Sophiatown play. The setting, Queeny's shebeen – a small
room with two door exits, one to the street outside, one to
the kitchen within – remains the same throughout; the
action takes place over twenty-four hours. Much of the
two-act play consists of a two-hander between Queeny and
Johnny, anticipating the 'Port Elizabeth' plays of the next
decade (*The Blood Knot*, *Hello and Goodbye* and *Boesman
and Lena*), all two-handers. The central conflict too –
between two people whose images of each other fail to
coincide with reality – becomes a familiar theme. As he
narrows down his focus, Fugard begins to discover his
method. At first, *Nongogo* seems as much in the naturalistic mode – he called it the 'tough neorealism' of the
American school[8] – as its predecessor. The shebeen
ambience – Queeny ruling her 'house' in abrasive style,
telling Sam she is boss and will determine her own terms of
business, throwing out the drunken father-to-be, Patrick –
is finely caught, to begin with. This has been developed in
later productions: for instance, by Barney Simon's 'The
Company' in a recent (1981) version at the Laager studio

theatre in the Market Theatre complex in Johannesburg. The cast, headed by two up-and-coming African performers, Thoko Ntshinga and Ramolao Makhene, introduced a new layer of authentic township slang from Soweto to update the dialogue; and the audience were obliged to clamber over boxes of 'empties' in a narrow passageway before entering the shebeen world of the play. Director and actress found it necessary to 'research' the lives of the still-active shebeen queens to obtain this authenticity;[9] Fugard and his cast knew it all only too well, as they knew the central dilemma of the 'queens' – women who had found some personal and financial independence, but yet who also might yearn for the traditional husband and family, for 'respectability'.

But to stress the naturalistic surface of *Nongogo* in this way allows audiences to miss the point – as if the play offers no more than a slice of authentic township life. There were complaints of distortion and exaggeration from the black audience at the first performance, complaints provoked by the final scene, which takes us beyond surface realism, as Queeny reveals her past and confronts Johnny.[10] It is highly 'theatrical', almost operatic. Lewis Nkosi observed at the time that, although this moment offered 'a deeply stirring exploration' of a shebeen queen's consciousness, *Nongogo* could have taken place anywhere, and did not arise 'out of *our* social experience'.[11] Of course not. Once again, Fugard imposes upon what he has observed of township life his own concerns: when Johnny realises that the woman who has taken him up and whom he hopes will become part of his newly 'respectable' life hides a secret as 'filthy' as his own, he is made to confess that 'sometimes I get the crazy idea that a man can change the world he lives in. Hell! You can't even change yourself.' Similarly, when Queeny is driven by Johnny's increasingly drunken despair into confessing the 'truth' about herself, about being a 'Non-gogo' and soliciting among the lines of mineworkers queuing for pay, she takes us out of the naturalistic dimension, exploding in a cry of self-lacerating rage when Johnny asks, 'Why did I have to think you were different?'

> QUEENY. Different from what? the respectable people out there? Respectable? They were my customers . . . the ones that lived cleanest and hated filth . . . like you! I've found Bibles in their pockets when they lay sleeping in my bed, with pictures of their pretty wives and nice clean children. And I bet Daddy took them all to church on Sundays.
>
> JOHNNY. Don't drag everything into the gutter with you, Queeny.
>
> QUEENY. I'm not the landlord of that strip of muck, Johnny. Everybody owns a plot down there.
>
> JOHNNY. Some of us try to crawl out of it.
>
> QUEENY. What do you think I've been doing for five years? It had ended, Johnny, it was dead and buried when you walked in here. But you won't let it stay that way, will you? . . . You've performed a miracle, Johnny. The miracle of Jesus and the dead body. You've brought it back to life. The warmth of your hate, the breath of your disgust has got it living again. I'm not too old . . . not *too* fat . . . .

And she laughs, walking up to Johnny 'provocatively', which drives him out. Crude and exaggerated as it is, the moment nevertheless provides the summing-up 'image' of the play. Queeny is wearing the scarlet dress bought to show Johnny what she will do for him, a visual irony which picks up the earlier whipping on and off of the red tablecloth he has brought into the shebeen. He told her earlier that 'red is your colour'; it is indeed, and she cannot escape it, any more than Johnny can face the implications of her attractiveness to him.

Yet Fugard does not only manipulate his black characters so as to test his own interest in the individual potential for change in a world of distressingly limited circumstances. The outrage which he felt in witnessing the daily lives of the people of Sophiatown leads him occasionally to a deeper truth, touched on in Queeny's final outburst: 'I can also tell you a few things about compounds, Johnny . . . .' The experience of sexual humiliation which has destroyed both of them has a common source; the gold mines. This is a reality which dominated – as it continues to dominate – the lives and aspirations of everyone, black and white. From the time Johannesburg came into being as a result of the discovery of gold on the Rand, the mining-industry has been central to the South African economy, and the manner of its exploitation central to its structure. The 'compounds' into which the miserable millions have been herded, peasants from all over Southern Africa separated from their wives and children and homes – this is what lies behind Johnny and Queeny, and which has stained everything they do. Fugard recognises more than he is fully aware of, which is why naturalism is ultimately inadequate for his purposes.

4
'Three Port Elizabeth Plays' and 'People Are Living There'

The Blood Knot began, and performances still begin, as an evocation of place. The opening entry of Fugard's first notebook, dated London 1960, reads,

> Korsten: The Berry's Corner bus, then up the road past the big motor-assembly and rubber factories. Turn right down a dirt road – badly potholed, full of stones, donkeys wandering loose, Chinese and Indian grocery shops – down this road until you come to the lake. Dumping ground for waste products from the factories. Terrible smell. On the far side, like a scab, Korsten location. A collection of shanties, pondoks, lean-to's. No streets, names, or numbers. A world where anything goes . . . . In one of these shacks the two brothers – Morrie and Zach . . . .[1]

Morris and Zach are two 'Coloured' sons of the same mother, outcasts tormented by the fact that one of them (Morris) is whiter, more 'European' than the other. *The Blood Knot* explores the shifting pattern of dominance and dependence between them created by this difference in a racialist society. The play which made Fugard's name at home and abroad, it set the pattern for the works which were to follow. Its inspiration, setting, dialogue and texture are essentially local: Korsten is a 'non-white' shantytown on the northern fringe of Port Elizabeth. Almost all Fugard's succeeding works are set in or around this place – most notably, the next two major plays, *Hello and Goodbye* and *Boesman and Lena*, which, with *The Blood Knot*, were subsequently published abroad as *Three Port Elizabeth Plays* (1974).

A less propitious place for the production of works of art or literature than Port Elizabeth it would be hard to imagine. Fugard has travelled widely, in order to perform in or direct (often both) his work; but he always returns to Port Elizabeth, literally and metaphorically. What is it about the place that grips and inspires him? Certainly it is very representative of South Africa. Nearly half a million people live there, two-thirds of whom are classified 'non-white', including mainly Africans, but also Chinese, Indians and 'Coloureds' (persons of mixed race). All 'non-whites' are obliged by law to live in 'locations' or 'townships' on the fringes of the city, but near its major industries, the most important of which is the motor-car industry. The poorer whites reside in northern suburbs such as Algoa Park, which adjoin the factories and 'non-white' areas; they are almost all Afrikaans-speaking. Wealthy whites, both Afrikaans- and English-speaking, live luxuriously in the tree-lined southern suburbs, near the beach. Apart from their servants (average two per household), garden 'boys', clerks and messengers, whites have next to no personal contact with blacks. Nor do the heavily censored media offer any effective exposure to black aspirations. As for 'culture', the whites attend drive-in cinemas and, occasionally, a visiting overseas theatre production; blacks make their own entertainment, in church or community halls. 'Liberals' are conspicuously absent, and most whites support the government and its apartheid policies. Blacks are left to extra-parliamentary forms of opposition, such as (increasingly) trade unions, and underground resistance.

'Can one be moved', asked Camus, 'by a city where nothing attracts the mind, where the very ugliness is anonymous, where the past is reduced to nothing? Emptiness, boredom, an indifferent sky, what are the charms of such places?' His answer is Fugard's too: 'Doubtless solitude and, perhaps, the human creature.'[2] All three 'Port Elizabeth' plays expose the bleakness, poverty and degradation of life in and around Port Elizabeth; all three also hint the possibility of survival, even joy. The paradox is profound, and characteristic. 'Overwhelmed' by Camus's writings during the years of writing these plays (1960–8), Fugard follows him to the brink of despair, where, nevertheless, may be found 'finally the only certainty, the flesh': living 'without hope, without appeal', without the traditional certainties of religion or history, we may be able to continue after all, relying on (in a favourite phrase from Camus) 'truths the hand can touch'.[3]

One of these 'truths' is that we are indissolubly bound, one to the other, by ties of blood or love. The title of the first play in the series, *The Blood Knot*, announces the theme; it also suggests the private, even intimate emphasis of these plays, all of which concentrate upon two characters in a tight, passionate and tormented relationship which only indirectly reflects the South African situation. Fugard himself felt on completion of his three 'Port Elizabeth' plays that they could be considered to form a trilogy called 'The Family': 'First brother and brother [*The Blood Knot*], then child and parent [*Hello and Goodbye*], and now in *Boesman and Lena*, parent and parent, man and woman.'[4] In the first two plays, parent figures – the mother in *The Blood Knot*, the father in *Hello and Goodbye* – hover invisibly off-stage, inspiring conflicting emotions of love, hate and fear; in *Boesman and Lena*, the two protagonists are parents alone and childless, but the mysterious appearance of an elderly black man implies claims of kin. 'Outa', as he is called (a term of familiarity and respect used by children towards elderly Africans), is the only representative of the great mass of black people in these plays, which ignore the 'township' experience so vividly if incompletely suggested in *No-Good Friday* and *Nongogo*. Fugard's main interest in these Port Elizabeth plays lies in other, more marginal groups: the 'Coloured' (*The Blood Knot* and *Boesman and Lena*) and the 'poor white' (*Hello and Goodbye*) – those whose identity seems most questionable, insecure.

The underlying private 'dynamic' of these plays is essential for their effect; it enables audiences to identify with the discarded, 'fringe' characters whose lives they portray. But it also distinguishes them from the series of plays which arose out of Fugard's almost simultaneous, ten-year involvement with the African men and women of New Brighton township, Port Elizabeth, who became the Serpent Players. The two most powerful and successful works in this series were published in *Statements* (1974): *Sizwe Bansi Is Dead* and *The Island*. With *Three Port Elizabeth Plays* and the third play in *Statements* (*Statements after an Arrest under the Immorality Act*), these works

established Fugard's reputation as a major modern dramatist. But the *Statements* plays, projects rooted in the
collaborative exercises begun with Serpent Players in 1963,
deserve separate, and later discussion. The three 'Port
Elizabeth' plays represent an earlier phase in his career – a
phase more personal, domestic and conventional in origin.

'Conventional' is, of course, a relative term. The point is,
the three 'Port Elizabeth' plays reflect a different conception of theatre from that of the *Statements* plays: crudely,
one may call it the theatre of Beckett, since Beckett is the
most obvious, immediate influence upon *The Blood Knot*
and its successors, as critics have been quick to notice. But
it is Beckett domesticated, localised. Like *Waiting for
Godot*, all three plays reveal two outcasts in a drab,
minimal setting, engaged in endless cross-talk, suggesting
an image of the absurdity of the human condition. But
Fugard's most powerful moments, his most memorable
images, take us beyond the private *Angst* in which they are
rooted without necessarily moving into the metaphysical:
his purpose is more specific, more social, more political,
than Beckett. Many reviewers and critics, especially in
South Africa, preferred to emphasise the moral and
'universal' at the expense of the social and political –
convenient for preserving the status quo in that country, as
well as involving a distortion of the plays' intent and effect.

Fugard admitted that he did not 'necessarily' consider
these plays to be 'political'; nevertheless,

> I try to relate the very real issues of today to my plays.
> Perhaps you could describe it as 'theatre of defiance';
> yes, my object is to defy. I am protesting against the
> conspiracy of silence about how the next man lives and
> what happens to groups other than our own.[5]

That last phrase is a giveaway: there is a sense in which he is always a white South African talking to other white South Africans; on the other hand, his work goes beyond the limitations this implies, as the three 'Port Elizabeth' plays reveal. The 'conspiracy of silence' to which Fugard refers characterised the 1960s in South Africa, the period immediately following the Sharpeville massacre. Opposition was silenced as the authorities demonstrated their determination not to be swayed from their chosen course: imprisonment, bannings, enforced exile, censorship or simple intimidation ensured that only those courageous, cunning or lucky enough were heard. The government, led by Dr Hendrick Verwoerd, introduced a more thorough-going and systematic form of apartheid than before, while taking ever-more drastic measures, with the help of Justice Minister John Vorster, against remaining opponents. The infamous 'Ninety-day' law was introduced, empowering the detention of suspects without charge and incom-municado. The black political parties, the ANC and the Pan African Congress, banned in the immediate aftermath of Sharpeville, turned to unlawful, violent protest: Umkhonto we Sizwe (Spear of the Nation) and Poqo (Pure, i.e. purely for Africans), offshoots of the ANC and PAC respectively, began acts of sabotage – the main effect of which was to increase support for the government among the whites, with the tiny exception of the remaining 'liberals', some of whom tried to show solidarity with the blacks by engaging in sabotage as well. Meanwhile South Africa became a republic, after being forced to leave the Commonwealth as a result of its racial policies. The 'winds of change' were sweeping down the continent, as country after country became independent of its colonial masters; only Rhodesia and the Portuguese colonies continued open

support for what became an isolated country, acknowledged to be a threat to world peace.

What could be done? Fugard, in London when the news
of Sharpeville and 'those appalling pictures' came through,
felt an urge to return, as 'an act of solidarity' with the
situation.[6] He did not in fact do so until nine months later,
by when his wife was pregnant, they had run out of money,
work and opportunity, and *The Blood Knot* had begun
growing in his notebooks. Finally written 'as a compulsive
and direct experience' on his return home to Port
Elizabeth, it was a play to defy the ruling racialist ideology,
expressed with such brutal clarity at Sharpeville. As we
have seen, the play revolves around the difference between
two 'Coloured' brothers – a difference defined as racial in
the most obvious, visual way ('Zachariah is dark-skinned
and Morris is light-skinned' according to the stage direction), but also in psychological, social, even cultural terms.
Morris's light skin has enabled him to 'pass for' white; he is
also prudent, controlled, literate, and his most important
possessions are a Bible and an alarm clock – both of which
he uses to impose 'order' upon his brother and himself.
Zachariah, by contrast, is dark-skinned, spontaneous, sen-
sual, illiterate; he earns their keep as some sort of park
attendant or factory watchman (the details are kept vague),
while Morris tends house, saves for their 'future', and
attempts to impart the 'civilised' virtues of routine, discussion and brotherly love. The two live together in a domestic
arrangement in which Morris's superior articulacy – expressed as a flow of ideas, words, quotations – commands
his brother's respect even as it robs him of the opportunity
for immediate satisfaction ('Golden Moments at two bob a
bottle'). The breadwinner is thus kept subservient. An
illusory dream of a future two-man farm is held out by

Morris as a way of escaping their squalid shack in Korsten.

The poverty of their world, 'a patchwork of scraps of corrugated iron, packing-case wood, flattened cardboard boxes, and old hessian bags, highlights the pathos of the opening moment, as Morris prepares Zach's footbath, and reinforces our sense of the importance of the trivial, the everyday, while it offers an irresistibly enjoyable, 'natural' entry into the main action. Most of Fugard's plays begin in this 'low-key', apparently makeshift, naturalistic manner. Morris's initial action suggests a domestic, servile role; but, as Zach relaxes and begins musing over the life he enjoyed before his brother's return, it emerges that the relationship is not so simple. To keep Zach under his spell, Morris tries to persuade him to take up with 'a corresponding pen-pal of the opposite sex', instead of a real woman. This leads to the 'appearance' of Ethel Lange of Oudtshoorn in their lives: 'eighteen years old and well-developed', she wishes to correspond with 'a gent of sober habits and a good outlook on life'. But Morris's little plan backfires: to his horror, Ethel turns out to be white; moreover, Zach likes the thought of 'this little white Ethel better than our future, or the plans, or getting-away, or foot-salts, or any other damned thing in here'. Not for long, however: Ethel intends to come on a visit to Port Elizabeth, and it is Zach's turn to be frightened. Morris warns him: 'They don't like these games with their whiteness'.

ZACHARIAH. What have I done, hey? I done nothing.
MORRIS. What have you thought? That's the question. That's the crime.... And what about your dreams.... All they need for evidence is a man's dreams.

At this point the play opens momentarily into the world of detentions and interrogation; but then we return to the relationship between the two brothers.

Zach, reversing his earlier role, thinks of a way out: Morris can stand in for him, and 'play white'. He takes the money Morris has put by for their 'future' and buys 'an outfit for a gentleman'. 'There's more to wearing a white skin than putting on a hat', objects his brother; 'this whiteness of theirs is not just in the skin, otherwise . . . well, I mean . . . I'd be one of them, wouldn't I?' Zach persists, and Morris reveals that he once 'tried for white', but was driven by his shame and guilt to return to Korsten and his darker brother – a revelation anticipated by a dream-like monologue at the end of Scene i, during which he wraps himself in the sleeping Zach's coat, trying to penetrate his brother's smell, his flesh, his pain. The penultimate scene of the play consists of another dream monologue, this time by Zach, who addresses his mother while Morris sleeps: 'Whose mother were you really?' he asks, plaintively; 'I got beauty . . . too . . . haven't I?' But these secret yearnings for recognition, for dignity and acceptance, are dispelled by the concluding scene, in which the discovery that their white pen-pal will not after all be coming leads the brothers into their last, and most dangerous game. Morris pretends to be white, indifferent, and arrogant; Zach plays the servile black. But things get out of hand: the 'simple, trustworthy type of John-boy' turns on his 'baas', threateningly – the ring of their alarm-clock catches Zach on the point of violence, standing above the praying, cringing 'white man'.

Fugard does not leave us with that climactic, warning image, heavy with implication as it is. 'What is it Morrie? The two of us . . . you know . . . in here?' asks Zach as they return to 'normality'. 'Home', Morris answers. 'Is there no other way?' 'No', replies Morris, in the last words. 'You see, we're tied together, Zach. It's what they call the blood knot . . . the bond between brothers.' With this utterance, we are left where we began: the two brothers in their Korsten shack at the end of the day.

The title and concluding words of *The Blood Knot* suggest a simpler, more explicit play than Fugard actually wrote, or than performance usually embodies. The first performance was, as we've seen, especially rich – in itself, and as an event. Undoubtedly part of the reason for the phenomenal initial success was the impact of Fugard and Mokae as performers: all reports confirm they gave an electrifying rendition of Fugard's script, developing and modifying it as they continued, so as to bring out ever more powerfully the subtle possibilities of pace and rhythm involved in their duet – elements it is not always easy to find in the printed text, which now seems somewhat overlong, and, at times, clumsy and repetitive, as Fugard himself freely acknowledges. But the power and conviction of his and Mokae's performance transcended the play's flaws, vindicating Fugard's belief in the importance of the 'pure theatre experience', the transmission of 'Truth' in a way and with a force unique to drama, by using nothing more than 'the actor and the stage, the actor on the stage'.

But what also captured those first audiences was the fact that here was a new, indigenous South African play, which explored the basic 'truth' or issue – race – yet which did so with immense passion, humour and pathos, and 'without ever mentioning that it is a problem or a political issue', as a reviewer in the liberal *Rand Daily Mail* put it. This brings us to a problem with the play: it permits, if it does not encourage, a naïvety of response which in South Africa, although not only there, leads to a separation of 'politics' and reality. James Ambrose Brown, one of South Africa's foremost theatre critics and a fellow playwright, was almost overwhelmed by *The Blood Knot*, but praised its 'lack of heat and anger when dealing with a subject which usually generates unbridled propaganda'; Bernard Levin, responding to the British production at the New Arts in Hampstead in February 1963, when Fugard was replaced by Ian Bannen, said, 'this is not a play about the "race problem" in ordinary terms at all, but a play about human beings caught in a tragic and inevitable fact'; and Kenneth Tynan, in a devastating notice of the same production which all but killed it for British audiences for the time, remarked that it merely reflected white South African guilt, 'but to people who would not be horrified if their daughter married a negro, it seems drably unadventurous'.[7]

What these reviewers and their attitudes reveal is not so much a 'conspiracy of silence', perhaps, as a refusal to acknowledge the social and political dimension of the play. *The Blood Knot* is not 'propaganda', or political in the narrow sense of dealing explicitly with public, identifiable events, personalities or policies; but, equally obviously it does deal with 'the very real issues of today', protesting 'about how the next man lives and what happens to groups other than own'. Like all of Fugard's plays, indeed, *The Blood Knot* reflects an experience, a society, in which to deny the congruence of individual, social and political aspects of life is to play right into the hands of the authorities. It is precisely the false compartmentalising of people and their thoughts which serves the ruling ideology, and permits it to continue. It was the more racially and politically aware American audience which seemed quicker to respond to early productions of *The Blood Knot* in these terms: Howard Taubman in the *New York Times* observed of the Cricket Theatre production there in 1964 that audiences should not think 'that what Mr Fugard reveals of the souls of white and black brothers living uneasily together involves only South Africa', while other critics found a tremendous insight in the last, shocking 'game' when Zach turns the tables on Morris. By embodying what he sees as the 'truth' of his 'place' in his work, Fugard cannot help but also embody its politics.

The Blood Knot reveals the impossibility of segregating, without cruelty and violence, people arbitrarily defined as 'different'. But it also suggests an acceptance of inhumanity and prejudice as permanent features of life. Fugard's Camus-derived 'metaphysic', his concern to examine the 'self' in the hell of everyday existence, allows him to escape proposing change. It is not so much that change is too frightening to contemplate, arousing images of interracial and fratricidal violence, although that is partly what lies behind the end of the play; but rather that his own sense of the individual's relationship to society and to history is fundamentally pessimistic. The repetitive, circular structure of *The Blood Knot* itself reinforces the play's conclusion: each of the first four scenes opens with Zach's return from work; the fifth and sixth break this pattern, reflecting the appearance of Ethel Lange in their lives, but are themselves mirror images of each other, the fifth taking place at midday, the sixth, midnight; with the seventh and last scene, Morris is preparing to leave and the shack appears to be in a state of disorder preparatory to change, but then we return to the beginning, since, after all, he remains where he is. The nightmare park fantasy is defined by a shift in lighting, emphasising the significance of the climactic image, the black man above and behind the cringing, praying white; but then we return to 'normality'.

To describe *The Blood Knot* in these terms may obscure the important element of humour in the play. Paradoxically, the bleak world created by Fugard is lit by moments of transcendence, moments when the discarded, confused scraps of everyday existence take on a new, almost lyrical quality. These moments are defined by language, gesture and image. Thus Morris looks out of the window onto the foul-smelling lake, sees its calmness, like 'a face without feeling', and notices the birds 'so white and beautiful' flying about then settling on it, without getting 'dirty'; or Zach remembers calling on a woman named Hetty to borrow a candle because someone was dying, 'So I stood in the street, very shy, and called: "Hetty . . . Hetty!" ' and she came to the window 'because she liked the sound', and took him and 'taught' him. Morris's tendency to pick up his Bible and read out a passage punctuates the action and reveals as it confirms his Calvinist conscience; but on one occasion, before the brothers go to sleep, he chooses 'Matthew. I like Matthew. (*Reads*.) "And Asa begat Josaphat, and Josaphat begat Joram, and Joram . . ."' – the familiar, interminable list never fails to raise a laugh, even as it reminds us that this is a play about the consequences of 'begetting'. When Morris and Zach take themselves back to their childhood, and all the humiliations of being a *Capie* ('Coloured') or *Kaffertjie* (little black 'Kaffir') return, they also recall their one special game: 'Just me and you', says Morris, 'I'll give you a clue. Toot-toot. Toot-toot', and they re-enact their joint fantasy, which transformed a scrapped car into their very own speedster, taking them faster and faster, until suddenly they drove into a flock of butterflies. The potential for human survival, even dignity, is always there. It was there, too, in the Sophiatown plays; but these were written in a language, and a manner, too unspecific and too unfamiliar to Fugard to allow this discovery; discovering his Port Elizabeth idiom, he discovers the source of a creativity rooted in the mundane, the trivial, the 'rubbish' of life.

In 1963, on his return to Port Elizabeth after the South African tour of *The Blood Knot*, Fugard wrote a play called

People Are Living There, 'an aberrant work', an almost 'literal transcription' of his experience of a Johannesburg boarding-house, without, 'seemingly, a socio-political context of any significance'. The central character of the two-act play, Milly, was the first of a series of attempts to invest in a single character (always a woman) 'the possibility of affirmation in an increasingly morbid society'.[8] The invisible catalyst of the action, and an ambivalent presence throughout, is Milly's lodger–lover, Ahlers, who has decided that, after ten years, it is time to try his chances elsewhere, since she is fifty and 'not a woman any more'. In revenge, Milly persuades her other male lodgers – Shorty, an incompetent postman and amateur boxer who raises silkworms when not being humiliated by his repressed child bride Sissy, and Don, a pimply, pseudo-intellectual cynic – to join her and 'have a good time'. As the evening unravels, their longings and disappointments emerge until, at the climax, Milly cries out,

> You are telling me this is all I get?
> DON. Yes!
> MILLY. Then somebody's a bloody liar. . . . Who wants to get up tomorrow if this is it? If this is all?

If she reaches despair, Milly also discovers that, simply, she is still alive and, the implication is, will survive. The quality of that survival remains questionable, as it does in all Fugard's plays; but here we question it in terms of its dramatic effectiveness, rather than in terms of the possibility as such of individual survival in a world of squalid, dehumanising circumstances. The reason is that, despite Fugard's tight focus in *People* upon a single evening in the lives of his impoverished, lonely and frustrated group, he had not found that single, generative image or complex of images which, in *The Blood Knot*, for example, holds the play together and gives the impression of a fusion of interests, rather than a somewhat miscellaneous collection of themes. Without that element of deep responsiveness to his own, specific environment, to Port Elizabeth, Fugard's work seems to lose pressure. In *The Blood Knot*, everything connects with the two men tied together in that tormenting relationship – even such apparently arbitrary details as the alarm clock which Morris uses to time his actions at the start, and which, fortunately for him, interrupts Zach when the latter is about to strike him, at the end. But, in *People Are Living There*, our awareness of time, and the gathering momentum of the evening, is signalled by such devices as Don, the callow existentialist and all too evidently Fugard's alter ego, tapping on the table with his pipe, while remarking the 'passing seconds': 'The sound of doom, Milly. Seconds becoming minutes, minutes becoming hours, days, months, years . . . .' It is tempting to respond as Milly does, with a snort of bored disgust; and, of course, we are meant to, up to a point. But there are other, more effective ways of suggesting the deep fear of time passing, of the meaninglessness of life in the face of mortality, a fear which weaves its way throughout the plays. There are moments, flashes of brilliant theatricality, which light up *People Are Living There* – as when Milly, in the dishevelled nightdress she resolutely refuses to change, but wearing Shorty's boxing-gloves to keep her hands warm, takes a swipe at the 'little bugger' out of rage which turns into enjoyment. But *People* lacks the coherence, the complexity, and the *point*, of the 'Port Elizabeth' plays.

The characters of *People* – no less than four, which also makes the play 'aberrant' – are 'poor white'. Their position is summed up tellingly by Don. 'Overseas you'd be a labourer', he tells Shorty. 'Here we have Natives to do the dirty work. You're saved by your white skin.' According to André Brink (in *Mapmakers*, 1983), the audience jumped to their feet and shouted 'Yes!' at this point during one production; but in fact the play barely suggests, much less attacks, the 'poor white'. In any case, for Fugard the 'poor white' Afrikaner who features in so much of his work is an object of pity rather than contempt, for understanding rather than condemnation. This he goes on to show in *Hello and Goodbye*, the second of his three 'Port Elizabeth' plays.

Hello and Goodbye is a harrowing account of the brief return home to the cramped family cottage at 57a, Valley Road, Port Elizabeth, of Hester Smit, ostensibly to get her share of the money she believes her crippled father received as compensation for his accident many years before. The play explores another 'blood knot': like Morris, she has returned to her brother (whom she finds alone), at least partly out of guilt for leaving; but this time it is the one who stayed at home who is the introspective neurotic, unable to take on work, while she is the unreflecting, spontaneous, less educated sibling. The structure and development of *Hello and Goodbye* is much tighter and more controlled than *The Blood Knot*; and the play may thus be summarised quite briefly.

It opens with Johnnie alone in the kitchen, tapping out the time passing on the side of a glass, wondering if he is going mad, and trying to avoid thinking about his father's recent death. He has been the mere adjunct of his crippled father, whom he has served as housekeeper and then as nurse during his last, bed-ridden years. When his sister appears, he seems at first not to recognise her. She has come home after fifteen years, having heard that her father is at death's door. Johnnie will not allow her to disturb their father, who, he leads her to believe, is resting in the next room. Goaded by her brother's evasions and pieties, she confesses she has become a prostitute: 'You want a sin? Here's one. I *Hoer*.' On condition that she will never return, Johnnie permits her to search through all the family relics for the compensation money she believes will enable her to change her name and live in a posh hotel. The boxes and suitcases are all brought out and opened, until the stage is littered with their possessions, and the whole mean past of the 'second-hand Smits of Valley Road' has been revealed. But no compensation. In one moment Hester discovers both that her hope is to be disappointed and that her father is already dead. She attacks her brother, knocking him to the floor in her rage: 'More! Explode! Swallow me up!' he exclaims, echoing the words he used to describe the explosion which mutilated his father. Hester apologises, and urges her brother to leave, and come with her to Johannesburg: 'Get a job, a girl, have some good times'. But he remains prone until she departs; then, in a macabre and chilling conclusion, he struggles up onto his father's crutches, and assumes the dead man's story even as he assumes his identity. 'Let's face it, a man on his own two legs is a shaky proposition.' We are left with this image of him, standing facing us, uttering the ultimate bitter irony, as darkness descends: 'Resurrection'.

The religious overtones are central. Johnnie's failed rebirth represents the failure of the Afrikaner to escape his own distorted faith, his Calvinist history. It is a faith, and a history, shared by those he denies. Just as the 'Coloured' Morris in *The Blood Knot* returns compulsively to the word of the Bible in a vain attempt to understand the 'retribution' exerted upon him for trying to be white, so Johnnie returns compulsively to his father's faith in providence to justify his weakness and suffering. When the railway construction line on which his father was working had reached Graaff-Reinet, 'the Lord's purpose in all suffering was revealed. Because there he met Mommie. "I was there in the wilderness – like Moses. The sleepers bent my back, the Lord bent my spirit. But I was not broken. It took dynamite to do that!" Hey?' 'Don't make me sick', is Hester's curt reply. Unlike Johnnie, she has renounced both God and Father, or so she believes: 'all our life it was groaning and moaning and what the Bible says and what God's going to do and I hated it! . . . I got so sick of it I went away.'

Hester hates her father, her memories, and the whole 'respectable' world. Yet, when the first of the family boxes has been lugged in by her brother, and opened, she realises she cannot reject everything; she pulls out a dress:

HESTER. Mommie. Smell, man. It's Mommie's smell.
JOHNNIE. (*smelling the dress*). I can't remember.
HESTER. I'm telling you, it's her. I remember. How do you like that, hey? All these years. Hell, man, it hurts. Look, I claim this too . . . .

Her search for the 'compensation' becomes a search for her childhood, for the feelings generated by memory and long suppressed. Act I ends with Johnnie maliciously reminding her of what she came for; Act II (an hour later) opens with them both absorbed in childhood memories, Hester sitting on a suitcase, a photograph album open on her lap. The dream cannot last, however: she becomes more, not less, frustrated as the family mementoes and discarded clothes multiply, and spill out confusedly upon the stage. Everything she touches confirms the emotional as well as material poverty of her past, of the family's crippling spiritual inheritance.

But Johnnie is the one who remains self-deluding,

crippled by the grip of the past and religion. Hester survives, to say 'Hello and Goodbye'. This is most effectively dramatised when she cries out, 'THERE IS NO GOD! THERE NEVER WAS!', and unwittingly hurls her mother's dress onto the floor, where it joins the rest of the family's inheritance. She thus frees herself while her brother submits, a contrast embodied dramatically by her more forceful, increasingly independent actions during Act II, while her brother begins to toy with, then try out, his father's crutches. Hester's desire to know is ultimately an expression of her desire to *be* – herself, in all her unhappy, Johannesburg whore's existence; Johnnie becomes no more than a living ghost.

Johnnie's maundering evasiveness, his resignation, all too easily become tiresome in production, however; while Hester, especially as portrayed by perhaps her most successful performer, Yvonne Bryceland, sustains the play, celebrating the woman's ability to face the worst and come through. Other actresses, most notably Janet Suzman in her prize-winning performance for the King's Head Theatre production (with Ben Kingsley, London, 1973), have equally effectively expressed Hester's powerful combination of crude vulgarity and vulnerability, her courage in the face of despair; but it is Miss Bryceland who so far has hit most precisely the narrow, bigoted and yet vital 'poor white' Afrikaner quality the role demands (in the Space production subsequently brought to the Riverside Studios, London, and filmed by BBC TV, 1977–9).

For the play requires that local texture, that Port Elizabeth accent, to bring out fully the tragedy which grips this brother and sister, as it grips, in different but related ways, the brothers Morris and Zach. It is the tragedy of 'The Bad Years', the early thirties, when the world recession hit South Africa and what jobs there were were reserved for whites: 'And all the time the kaffirs sit and watch the white man doing kaffir work – hungry for the work. They are dying by the dozen!' And so will many more, is the implication, before the Afrikaner comes off his crutches, and loses that unique sense of continuing grievance which blinds him to the suffering of others.

Boesman and Lena seems to take us back to the first of the three 'Port Elizabeth' plays. Once again, we meet two 'Coloured' characters from Korsten, the 'non-white' shantytown in which Morris and Zach have their 'pondok'. But 'Boesman' (the name implies someone of mixed race which includes a touch of 'Bushman' blood) and his Lena (a 'Hotnot meid', i.e 'Coloured' servant woman with 'Hottentot' blood) are an even more marginal and wretched couple. Before the play's action begins, they have been evicted, their ramshackle Korsten home bulldozed to the ground. And the play opens with the starkest setting so far – the stage is 'empty'.

Into this empty space staggers Boesman, all his worldly possessions upon him: on his back an old mattress and blanket, a blackened paraffin tin, an apple box containing some cooking utensils, clothing and so on, in one hand a piece of corrugated iron, dragging noisily along the ground. He chooses a spot, drops his load, and waits. After a minute, a similarly burdened figure emerges from the darkness – Lena, a bundle of firewood under her arm, pots and pans on her head. Unwilling to interrupt her stiff-necked, precarious progress, she goes past him then pauses without turning her head: 'Here?' Boesman spits, says nothing. With the last of her strength, Lena allows her burden to fall, and squats down slowly, painfully. She rests, then works a finger between her toes: 'Mud! Swartkops!' They have reached the Swartkops river estuary, some seven miles north, on the very outskirts of Port Elizabeth.

1. Athol and Sheila Fugard with the African Theatre Workshop, Sophiatown, Johannesburg, 1958/9

2. Athol Fugard directing Zakes Mokae as Blackie in *Nongogo*, Johannesburg, 1959

3. Zach (Zakes Mokae) threatens Morrie (Ian Bannen) in *The Blood Knot* at the New Arts Theatre, London, 1963

4. Janet Suzman and Ben Kingsley in the RSC production of *Hello and Goodbye* at The Place, London, 1973

5. Athol Fugard as the servile Boesman in the film version of *Boesman and Lena*, directed by Ross Devenish, 1974

6. Athol Fugard rehearsing two Serpent Players (Mike Ngxcolo and George Mnci) in *Antigone*, Port Elizabeth, 1965

7. Athol Fugard watches Wilson Dunster (standing), Yvonne Bryceland (on the floor) and Val Donald preparing the scriptless, experimental *Orestes* in the Labia Rehearsal Room, Cape Town, 1971

8. Winston Ntshona and John Kani in *Sizwe Bansi Is Dead*, directed by Athol Fugard at The Space, Cape Town, 1972

9. Athol Fugard and Yvonne Bryceland in *Statements after an Arrest under the Immorality Act*, directed by Fugard at The Space, Cape Town, 1972

10. Sizwe Bansi has his 'snap' taken: The Space's 'South African Season' at the Royal Court, London, 1973/4

11. Winston Ntshona and John Kani in *The Island* at the Royal Court, London, 1973/4

12. Shelagh Holliday and Marius Weyers in the Market Theatre, Johannesburg, production of *A Lesson from Aloes*, 1978

As Stanley Kauffmann observed, this is a play in which *the ground* is important: 'On this mud, out of which we all come, Boesman and Lena make their camp.'[9] And this is almost the entire action of the play. Except that an elderly black man comes out of the dark to share their fire, and dies beside it. The pair take up their burdens again, and move on.

The minimal setting, sparse action and stripped-down dialogue suggest an extreme, a limit beyond which human endurance cannot go. Yet, by a profound paradox, it is at this limit that the possibility of hope, of survival, even joy, emerges. Despite herself, and all that she has suffered – at the hands of the white man, and her partner – Lena carries on; indeed, at the crucial moment, she finds herself beginning to sing, to dance, to stamp down on that mud. Her song celebrates, as it reflects, her miserable life, her mean existence:

> Korsten had its empties
> Swartkops got its bait
> Lena's got her bruises
> Cause Lena's a *Hotnot meid*.
>
> Kleinskool got prickly pears
> Missionvale's got salt
> Lena's got a Boesman
> So it's always Lena's fault.
>
> Coegakop is far away
> Redhouse up the river
> Lena's in the mud again
> *Outa*'s sitting with her.

The list of place names refers to her struggle, throughout

the play, to create meaning out of her existence by discovering the order in which she and Boesman have visited these poor little Port Elizabeth shantytowns. It is a struggle which provides the whole emotional impetus of the play, which is effectively *her* play, and which lives or dies according to the actress who performs her, and the authenticity with which her profound, driving need to be witnessed in her extremity is suggested.

To begin with, Lena cannot remember where she has been, or when; and Boesman taunts her cruelly by adding to her confusion. He is about to attack her physically when Outa (as Lena calls him) appears, to be repelled by Boesman on the grounds of his and Lena's racial superiority. His mere presence provokes Boesman into fits of futile jealousy. But Lena turns to the black man for sympathy and comfort, asking him to bear witness to her suffering – the beatings she has received, her miscarriages in the dark. She obtains permission from Boesman for the old man to remain the night by offering in exchange her only other solace, a bottle of cheap wine. Outa cannot speak or understand her language: he talks only his own, Xhosa (varied according to production and actor, but Xhosa is local to Port Elizabeth). Outa learns to repeat Lena's name, but she (and we) cannot make out anything else he says. His is a weary, melancholy tone, the tone of a man to whom nothing more can happen; he has seen all, suffered all. The first act ends as Boesman returns to the hovel he has made in order to get drunk, while Lena remains outside with her new companion, forbidden to join Boesman.

An hour later, in the second act, Boesman emerges drunk and attacks Lena, who responds with her mocking song and dance. Boesman then reveals that he broke the empty bottles earlier that day, for which she was beaten: 'I dropped the empties.' Why? Boesman hits himself in his self-loathing and disgust, parodies himself earlier in the day, when he cried out '*Ja, baas! Dankie baas!*', thanking the white man for destroying their pathetic Korsten hovel. 'We're whiteman's rubbish'; 'We're not people any more'. He hates Lena because he hates himself. Their attention turns to the old man; and they realise that, quietly and alone, he has died. In his death, the black man becomes their 'rubbish', and also a threat. Dimly realising this, Boesman attacks the corpse, hitting and kicking it, while Lena watches. It is a horrifying moment, touching the ugliness and fear, the gratuitous cruelty at the heart of their society, even as it suggests the impotence of the downtrodden, their helplessness in the face of white power. The two must move on before the body is discovered, and so they scrape together their pots and blankets, demolish their makeshift shelter, and leave – the black man remaining dead in the mud, as the two trudge silently off into the darkness.

Lena is defined by her pain; Boesman by his shame. They are caught between the white man who despises and rejects them, and the black who can sympathise but is in his own world of even deeper, incomprehensible suffering. When Boesman finally explains to Lena the towns and shanties and jobs that preceded Swartkops, she realises, 'It doesn't explain anything.' But there is more to their lives than the darkness from which they emerge at the beginning, and to which they return at the end: pain, shame, suffering; but also, fragmentarily, arbitrarily, joy. The play reminds us of the obstinate survival of humanity despite everything.

Boesman and Lena suggests the depths to which the human spirit can sink in South Africa: 'How do you throw away a dead *kaffer*?' It also suggests that people can survive, can express life. It does not reveal why, or how; any more than any of the other three 'Port Elizabeth' plays.

Ruminating upon the 'social content' of *Boesman and Lena*, Fugard felt 'nagging doubts', felt he was 'opting out' and 'not saying enough'; even though at one level the predicament of the 'Coloured' couple 'is an indictment', was this 'explicit enough'?[10] But explicitness belongs to a different kind of theatre, a kind of theatre he was to approach with *Sizwe Bansi is Dead* and *The Island*.

5
The 'Statements' Plays

Towards the end of *The Island*, the second of the three plays published in *Statements* (1974), a large, clumsy black man appears on stage in a wig of frayed rope, a necklace of nails, and a shirt stuffed with false breasts. He is pretending to be the ancient Greek princess Antigone. But we do not laugh. Nor do we laugh when he goes on to deliver Antigone's famous speech, defying the law which has condemned her. For what we are watching is a play-within-a-play: a two-man version of Sophocles's classic work performed by convicts before a prison audience in South Africa's maximum security centre for political offenders, Robben Island. Moreover, our reactions have been anticipated by an earlier scene in the play, during which Winston's first assumption of Antigone's wig and padding has his cell mate John – and us – falling about with laughter. 'You call laughing at me Theatre?' the big man exclaims, resentfully. 'Who cares', comes the reply. 'As long as they' (John sweeps his arm to include both imaginary and real audiences), 'as long as they listen at the end!'

By listening, we may be said to 'witness' the 'statement' made by the play. It is a statement about the injustice of the law which sends men to Robben Island for defying apartheid. But it is also a statement about 'Theatre'. *The Island* makes explicit, and asks us to recognise, the function of drama in a society of struggle and oppression. The play suggests that men may survive the most intolerable conditions if they are able to discover and articulate a meaning for their suffering – a meaning here offered by *Antigone*. In *The Island* a tradition is reactivated (as it was by Anouilh in Nazi-occupied France) which defies the law in the name of the conscience and dignity of man.

Unlike the 'Port Elizabeth' plays, the three *Statements* plays – *Sizwe Bansi Is Dead*, *The Island* and *Statements after an Arrest under the Immorality Act* – all testify to the nature and effects of specific apartheid laws: the pass laws; the laws banning the black opposition, the ANC and PAC; and the so-called 'Immorality Act' (Prohibition of Mixed Marriages Act, 1949). Inevitably, this new explicitness aroused misunderstanding, even hostility, from critics accustomed to find in Fugard's work 'universal', 'spiritual' values: Stanley Kauffmann, who praised these qualities in *Boesman and Lena*, saw *Sizwe Bansi* as 'superficial' and 'only about the troubles of South African blacks'. The *Listener* noted that the first two *Statements* plays 'call for political change, if not for revolutionary action, but they also make us aware that better political systems ultimately depend upon changes of heart'. [1]

But, as George Orwell once remarked, calling for a change of heart rather than a change of structure is *the* alibi of people who do not wish to endanger the status quo. Is this all the *Statements* plays do? The answer is complicated,

History of 1st performance

not least by the fact that the very process of creation behind the two plays, *Sizwe Bansi* and *The Island*, which were 'devised' by Fugard and the black actors John Kani and Winston Ntshona, was in defiance of the authorities, who, in turn, attempted to stifle performances. When *Sizwe Banzi* (original spelling) was first due to appear before an 'open', i.e. multiracial, audience at the Space in Cape Town in 1972, the police forced the management to cancel. And, when they reopened the next night as a (massively enlarged) 'club', two plain-clothes men attempted to intimidate the group, but without success. *The Island* could not be thus named for its early performances at the Space, where it appeared under the obscure but pointed (for those in the know) title, *Die Hodoshe Span*, i.e. 'Hodoshe's work-team', so named after a Robben Island warder called 'Hodoshe' (literally, 'carrion-fly'). *Sizwe Bansi*, as well as the name of a character, is a Xhosa phrase meaning 'the people are strong'. To avoid censorship, neither play was written down until production – and the recognition which followed – abroad. It is illegal to publish material about conditions upon 'the island' in any case.

When all three *Statements* plays appeared at the Royal Court in London as a 'South African Season' (1973–4), Fugard was accused by the South African cultural attaché of creating 'hundreds of enemies' for his country every night. But by then the astonishing success and attendant publicity gained by the plays had become protection for the playwright and his co-creators, action against whom would then have been an embarrassment outweighing the supposed negative effects of the plays themselves – as was proved when an international outcry forced the authorities to release Kani and Ntshona after imprisonment in the Transkei for anti-Bantustan remarks expressed as part of their performance there.

The third play in the collection, *Statements after an Arrest*, created for, and to some extent with, Yvonne Bryceland, who performed with Fugard in the first version (provided as the opening production of the Space in May 1972), Fugard regards as his own. Certainly it reflects a more private, inward impulse than the other two, anticipating the direction he was to take subsequently, in *Dimetos*; yet it is also, as its title suggests, a 'statement' – of what it means to live within, and try to survive, apartheid. Less direct than *Sizwe Bansi* or *The Island* and, unlike them, dealing with interracial rather than the 'black' experience, it has been less vulnerable to outside pressure. But, again, like the other two plays, it is a radical, 'extreme' work: both in terms of what it says, and how it goes about doing so.

All three *Statements* plays involve extensive mime, narrative disruption, nudity or physical 'exposure', surreal lighting-effects and direct addresses to the audience. This reflects a shift in Fugard's conception of theatre. The 'Port Elizabeth' plays were written in the conventional modern way to show the absurdity of life, the senselessness of ideals and purpose, despite which humanity struggles to survive. But these plays had been, he thought, 'so conventional', involving 'the *writing* of a play . . . *setting* that play in terms of local specifics . . . the actors *assuming* false identities' (Introduction, *Statements*). The *Statements* plays challenge this orthodox procedure, in favour of involving the creative abilities of the performers – their history, experiences, the very shape of their bodies. They are, in Grotowski's terminology, to sacrifice themselves to the spectators so as to inspire in their audience a similar process of psychic discovery – the whole event to take on the intensity and significance of a religious ritual. In the *Statements* plays, Fugard was attempting to participate in the international search for a new theatrical language, initiated by, amongst others, Peter Brook and Jerzy Grotowski. What he achieved was the expression of an everyday experience of suffering and protest by others, which helped ensure the continuity and survival of that protest. Black South African theatre groups whose work began to flourish in the townships from the early seventies testify to this, even as they press for a theatre more explicit and revolutionary than anything Fugard or his co-creators were capable of. Fugard's intervention may have been partial and contradictory; nevertheless it represents a unique attempt to respond to the lives of those from whom his background, upbringing and education (not to mention the laws of the land) were supposed to have excluded him.

How did all this come about? The answer lies in a complex and stirring series of events, the details of which are not yet (if they ever will be) altogether clear. A brief account must suffice. As we have seen, the story began early in 1963, shortly after Fugard's return home from the *Blood Knot* tour – a tour which had made that play and, especially, Zakes Mokae's role in it, a byword in the townships. The playwright was approached by a group of amateur drama enthusiasts in New Brighton, Port Elizabeth, with 'the old, old request', as Fugard confided to his notebooks; 'actually it is hunger. A desperate hunger for meaningful activity – to do something that would make the hell of their daily existence meaningful.'[2] Fugard felt he could not refuse, and so, under his experienced direction, the group (which included a clerk, two teachers, a busdriver and domestic servants) embarked upon a series of suitably adapted productions of 'classical' works – the first of which, Machiavelli's *The Mandrake*, was hailed locally as a masterpiece of improvisation.

Improvisation was the key to the Serpent Players' practice (their name derived from an abandoned snake pit in which they were offered a space to perform). Within two years, they had gone on to produce cheaply mounted 'township' versions of *Woyzeck, The Caucasian Chalk Circle, The Father* and *Antigone*, in venues such as St Stephen's church hall, without adequate lighting, seating, props or backstage facilities. Discussion–readings and rehearsals were held where possible after work – in a 'Coloured' kindergarten, or Fugard's own garage, to avoid the restrictions upon interractial activity. Rough working-conditions and the inevitable problems with the race laws were familiar to Fugard from his Sophiatown days. But this was not Johannesburg; and it was after Sharpeville, not before. Nelson Mandela had recently been arrested, and was soon to be convicted of sabotage and conspiracy to overthrow the government. The Players, their relatives and friends (including the Fugards) came under surveillance from the start. In December 1964, days before the opening of their Brecht play, Azdak (Welcome Duru) was arrested. Fugard took over the part, and the performance pro-ceeded. But within months three more members were arrested, including Norman Ntshinga, who was about to play Haemon in *Antigone*. A purge of the Eastern Cape – with its long tradition of black militancy – had begun.

Astonishingly, the Serpent Players did not collapse. Instead, a new phase of 'playmaking', without texts or identifiable authors, began. Brecht's *Messingkauf Dialogues* provided particular inspiration. But it was the events of the time which had overwhelming effect. When Fugard attended Ntshinga's trial (he was accused of belonging to one of the banned opposition movements), the playwright took the actor's wife, blues-singer Mabel Magada, along. She was recognised by an elderly man from New Brighton who had just been sentenced. He took off his coat (his only possession) and give it to her saying, 'Go to my home. Give this to my wife. Tell her to use it.'[3] This became the Players' first attempt to improvise a play directly out of their own experiences. The whole process was made visible in *The Coat* (1967), 'An Acting Exercise from the Serpent Players of New Brighton', as it was presented to its first audience, a white 'theatre-appreciation group' who had asked to see a sample of their work. They were expecting a comedy. But, since permission for a performance in a 'white area' had only been given on condition that it was not public, that the black actors did not use the toilets in the hall, and that the cast returned home immediately afterwards, the Players decided to put on *The Coat*, using their own names, and a Brechtian actor–presenter who encouraged spectators to think about, and not merely sympathise with, the experiences they were witnessing. From then on, the Serpent Players alternated 'classic' productions with similar improvisations – *Friday's Bread on Monday*, *The Last Bus* and *Sell-out*.

Meanwhile, two new members began to show particular promise: John Kani, who replaced the arrested Ntshinga in *Antigone* in 1965; and Winston Ntshona, an old schoolfriend of Kani's from New Brighton, whom he introduced to the group two years later. Both in their mid twenties, Kani a janitor in the Ford plant, Ntshona a factory laboratory assistant, the men were to have an extraordinary effect upon the depleted Players, their director Fugard, and the theatre. By 1972 they were appearing in their first major production, Camus's *The Just*, retitled *The Terrorists*, at the Space – an experience which led to a remarkable decision. In a country without black drama schools, professional theatre, or the least encouragement to write, direct or act, they decided to become full-time. They had to be classified as Fugard's domestic servants. Within months, their joint commitment issued in the collaborative work-shop productions *Sizwe Bansi* and *The Island*.

Fugard's involvement with the Serpent Players led him to recognise the importance of using the stage for a more immediate and direct relationship with the audience than had seemed possible with his own plays. Yet he felt that the 'facts', relevant as they were to the times, which formed the basis of the Players' work, lacked the 'density and ambiguity of truly dramatic images' (Introduction, *Statements*). After the South African tour of *Boesman and Lena*, and cut off from developments abroad by the withdrawal of his passport since 1967, he seemed to have reached an impasse. The arrival of Grotowski's *Towards a Poor Theatre*, along with notes taken at the Polish director's New York lectures by Barney Simon and Mary Benson, provided the necessary 'provocation' to develop the more extreme form of improvised, actors' theatre which emerged, almost at once, in the scriptless experiment *Orestes* (1971).

Orestes was developed in collaboration with Yvonne Bryceland and two other white actors in a concentrated spell of private rehearsals. It was based upon the Johannesburg-station bomb protest of 1964, an 'image' of which was 'superimposed' upon the 'image' of Clytemnestra and her two children, Orestes and Electra. In it, Fugard attempted to articulate the nature and effect of violence, encouraging the performers to use apparently trivial actions to suggest the deep, primitive roots of extreme events. A record of the experiment now rests in three large drawing-books, in the form of a 'score' and the developing 'exposures' of its limited, fringe run. The main significance of it lay in the opportunity it afforded Fugard of learning how to release the creative abilities of actors yet further than his work with the Serpent Players had so far permitted.

What Fugard did was to give his actors a 'mandate' – 'at least an image, sometimes an already structured complex of images' – to create a performance which, disciplined and repeated until 'fixed' in broad dramatic terms, became the play. The role of writer was not jettisoned, it was transformed. Fugard was now writing *'directly'* into the 'space and silence' of the stage (Introduction, *Statements*). The element of control and discipline maintained by the 'scribe–director' in this process distinguishes Fugard's work from the loose, not to say wildly indulgent practice of other late sixties theatre groups abroad, such as Julian Beck's Living Theatre – whose version of *Antigone* signally failed to turn its white middle-class American audiences into permanent revolutionaries, as was claimed it would. Unlike such works, which exploit liberal uneasiness and make exaggerated claims about the imminent collapse of British or American society, Fugard's *Statements* plays invite understanding, even compassion, rather than facile anger or self-indulgent guilt, while making it quite clear that there is no escape from politics. This is not to deny their limitations, which are the limitations of liberal humanism in the South African situation; nevertheless, as 'statements', they still defy the status quo.

The Island is the most persuasive example of this. It takes us into the heart of the suppressed black opposition, languishing on Robben Island, to affirm brotherhood: *'Nyana we Sizwe!'* The Xhosa rallying-cry ('Son of the land' or, simply, 'People') is uttered by Winston (played by Winston Ntshona) at two critical moments: when the two men help tend each other's wounds at the beginning of the play; and, just before their joint performance of 'The Trial and Punishment of Antigone' at the prison concert, when

Winston manages to overcome his resentment that John is to be released. The import is the same, and unmistakable: it is an expression of solidarity which will survive the disappearance of their oppressors. Fugard's continuing interest in the nature of the bonds which tie us one to another has never been more effectively politicised. This is what his collaboration with black actors has brought about. But it was *Sizwe Bansi Is Dead* which first revealed what the blend of creative talent, experience and responsiveness to the daily pains of ordinary black South Africans could provide in the theatre.

Sizwe Bansi began when Fugard came across a photograph of an African smiling broadly; Kani said no black South African would smile like that unless his passbook was in order; later, Ntshona noticed a studio photograph of a smiling man with a pipe in one hand and a cigarette in the other. These images became Fugard's 'mandate' to Kani and Ntshona, who added further details from their own lives, including what was to become the brilliant thirty-minute opening monologue from Kani as a photographer called Styles, who has (like Kani) worked in the Ford plant.

Sizwe Bansi consists of a complex web of monologues, played, as with the other *Statements* plays, entirely by two actors. Kani and Ntshona people their bare stage with what seems like the entire New Brighton community they know, in a *tour de force* of mime, improvised dialogue and remembered gesture. There are no conventional act or scene divisions; transitions are created by word, gesture and, most strikingly, lighting. A table, chair and simple props (camera, display board and a reversible map/cityscape) suggest Styles's studio. The play begins when the dapper young Styles enters his 'studio' and while waiting for business sits down to read his newspaper. He reads aloud from it, adding his own comments. The device defines his sagacity at the same time as it establishes contact with the audience. A news item about the Ford plant leads Styles to recall his days there, notably the preparations for a visit by 'Mr Henry Ford Junior number two'. The panic among the white bosses, the furious sweeping, washing and painting that ensues, and Styles's own role as 'translator' for the Afrikaans foreman, who urges the 'boys' to sing and smile while they work, are all re-enacted in graphic and hilarious detail. The climax of this sequence, which gives a very good idea of the dehumanising conditions of work in the plant, comes when 'Ford number two', the biggest boss of them all, walks in – and straight out again. Styles decides to leave and become his own boss: he has seen what it is like to fawn before others. So he sets up in business with his 'strong-room of dreams. The dreamers? My people. The simple people, who you never find mentioned in the history books.'

Just as we begin to wonder where all this is leading, Winston Ntshona enters. In contrast to Styles, he is hesitant, ill-at-ease. He has come for a 'snap' to send to his wife back in the Ciskei Bantustan. Styles prepares the man for entry into his 'dream' by seating him before the cityscape, a cigarette in one hand. Just as the photo is being taken, the man, beaming innocently, reaches into his pocket and produces his pipe – so that he seems to be smoking with both hands. The moment usually brings the house down. Like the greatest comedy, it is essentially simple – and sad, too: this rural illiterate will never realise his dream. Styles persuades him to have a 'movie' or action photograph; when the flash goes off, there is a blackout except for a single spot on 'Robert' (Ntshona), who dictates his letter to his wife, a device which reveals his history to us. His true name is Sizwe Bansi, and he recounts how he came to Port Elizabeth for the work unobtainable in the Bantustan. Lacking the necessary permit, he called on a man named Buntu for help. The play shifts yet again into a new dimension, and the scene in which Buntu (played by a sober, serious Kani) explains to Sizwe the consequences of not having a passbook in order.

This allows for a graphic account of the whole panoply of pass laws, labour permits, travel limitations, residence restrictions and so on which apply to black South Africans. 'Why is there so much trouble?' asks Sizwe, pathetically. Buntu's reply is to tell of the funeral of Outa Jacob, an itinerant farmworker left by his white employer to die: 'That's it brother. The only time we'll find peace is when they dig a hole for us and press our face to the earth.' Buntu then takes Sizwe to a 'shebeen' and, as they leave it, drunk, Buntu relieves himself on what he thinks is a pile of rubbish. But it is a dead man. He panics, but Sizwe cries out, 'Would you leave me lying there . . .?' Buntu, who can read, notices that the dead man's passbook is valid; so they take it, abandoning the body. This is Sizwe's chance; he can take on the dead man's identity. But Sizwe, drunkenly self-righteous and stubborn, does not want to surrender his name. He is a man, not a ghost. In demonstration, he lowers his trousers and grasps his genitals. But Buntu persuades him that it is better to lose his identity and, implicitly, his manhood, to survive. With Sizwe's photo pasted in it, Robert Zwelinzima's passbook becomes his own, and – 'Sizwe Bansi . . . is dead'. Buntu rehearses Sizwe in his new identity, taking on a variety of roles to ensure Sizwe can 'prove' he is Robert. The trick cannot keep him out of trouble for ever: 'Our skin is trouble.' But he will try it. The 'letter' comes to an end as 'Robert' returns to his 'movie' pose, Styles once again behind the camera, uttering the last words: 'Now smile, Robert. . . . Smile'. A camera flash and blackout fixes this final image in the audience's mind. But it

pg
28

is a deeply ironic image: we have been taken behind the black man's smiling face, and we now know what it hides.

John Kani reported that Fugard 'told us we need our art, not propaganda'.[4] There *is* propaganda in *Sizwe Bansi*: in the 'facts' of apartheid which are reported; in the assumption, plainly expressed, that only the blacks can help each other. Indeed, the liberal view that there is always another side to the question gets short shrift in these plays – as does a certain kind of liberal, when Styles mockingly refers to Buntu as someone always helping people: 'If that man was white they'd call him a liberal.' Of course Buntu *does* help; yet his help is no more than a temporary alleviation of the problem. *Sizwe Bansi* takes sides, suggesting that, even if survival is possible, life on these terms is questionable.

Nevertheless, any propaganda effect is subsumed within the art – which is primarily an art of performance. The actors and co-creators earned the plaudits with which they were showered (*Sizwe Bansi* brought them, amongst other awards, a joint 'Tony'). Kani and Ntshona seemed inseparable from *Sizwe Bansi*, which thereby gained an authenticity absent from other 'political' drama of the time. Does this mean that the play can only operate successfully with the actors who helped create it and whose experiences it embodied? Time will tell, although it has already proved possible for others to perform the work. Moreover, the first, predominantly white-liberal audiences in South Africa and abroad, whose favourable responses perhaps ensured quick and widespread acceptance, have been succeeded by, for example, a New Brighton audience in which there was a near-riot as people reacted 'with disbelief, panic and fear that these things were actually being talked about out loud and then there was joy, that this was a celebration of small things in their lives'.[5]

'Celebration' is an important word in Fugard's vocabulary. It highlights the humour, the intense enjoyment of simple pleasures, which lifts *Sizwe Bansi* and its immediate successor out of the bleakness and pessimism they also suggest. If *Sizwe Bansi* shows what everyday life is like for black township people struggling to survive, *The Island* shows what happens when, as they must, they fall into trouble. 'Our skin is trouble.' In both plays, acting a part is a means for survival: the boundaries between life and art are redrawn. Like *Sizwe Bansi*, *The Island* evolved out of the experiences of its co-creators. Not that either Fugard (who once again provided the initial 'mandate' in the form of accumulated notes and ideas about Robben Island) or Kani or Ntshona had ever been to the notorious prison. But they were told about it by the Serpent Players, notably Welcome Duru and Norman Ntshinga, who served time there; and about a two-man version of *Antigone* (the play in which he was about to perform when arrested) which Ntshinga arranged.

The Island opens with the wail of a siren. John and Winston (they use their own names) mime the digging of sand. They are dressed in khaki shorts, like the 'boys' their keepers would make them. Each loads a barrow, which he then wheels and empties just where the other is working. A strong light suggests pitiless surroundings. The only sounds are their grunts, and the ceaseless buzzing of flies. Their task seems endless, a Sisyphean image of life as pointless, interminable suffering. A shrill whistle stops them at last, and the two are shackled together, to run back to their tiny cell. All the action is confined to a small space on the floor: the stage provides a metaphor for their imprisonment. Back in their cell, they treat each other's injuries, John using the only available medicine for Winston's swollen eye – his own urine (in performance, literally).

Despite the anger towards their gaolers their punishment

arouses, the two men agree they are brothers – although the relationship is more like marriage, with John bustling about and nagging his slower, more reluctant partner. As in *Sizwe Bansi*, the 'natural' characters of the performers are exploited: John is pushful, resourceful, quick-witted; Winston slower, more vulnerable. So it is John who tries to persuade Winston to go through their version of the remembered play for the prison concert. At first Winston resists, as we have seen. After the laughter has died down, and John has explained that 'Theatre' is all they have, that failing to perform is just what their chief warder and unseen tormentor, Hodoshe, wants, John is suddenly taken away, to be told that his sentence has been reduced on appeal. Winston is stunned by the news, but it brings the two men together again. The third scene (unlike *Sizwe Bansi*, the play is structured in four scenes) reveals them trying to sleep, later the same night. Winston catches John counting the days he has left. 'Your freedom stinks, John, and it's driving me mad.' He seems to be sinking beneath the weight of his life sentence; but then he tells John to forget him – as he will forget John. Reaching the pitch of despair, he is able to pity the other man. And we know what kind of 'freedom' it is that awaits John: it is implicit in this play, as it is explicit in *Sizwe Bansi*.

The final scene provides the actual performance of 'The Trial and Punishment of Antigone', with the audience addressed as if in the prison. John, as Creon, explains he is the people's defender and protector against 'subversive elements', who must be judged and punished. He cross-examines Antigone (Winston), who pleads guilty, but who claims obedience to a law higher than Creon's. Sentenced to be immured on 'the island' for life, Winston then tears off his wig and confronts us as 'himself', uttering the last words uttered by Antigone in Sophocles's play: 'I go now to my living death, because I honoured those things to which honour belongs.' The play ends where it began, John and Winston shackled together, running, as a siren wails.

Winston cannot be saved, any more than his ancient, semi-mythical predecessor. But he has made his 'statement', and is unrepentant. Looming up through his concluding address, one can easily visualise the leader of another 'span' on Robben Island: Nelson Mandela, whose concluding speech in his own defence was based on the same premise as Winston's – and Antigone's. It is a speech no South Africans are officially permitted to read; but its spirit lives on. *The Island* is a powerful tragedy, with universal implications, for overseas audiences; for South Africans, its message is more direct, an expression of solidarity with their banned and imprisoned leaders.

Neither *Sizwe Bansi Is Dead* nor *The Island* calls for revolution. But their central characters endure, in defiance of the law. Fugard could go no further; indeed, it is unlikely he would have gone this far, without the joint commitment of the Serpent Players, whose 'statement' these plays witness. His next play, *Statements after an Arrest under the Immorality Act*, is altogether less overt, less political. Yet, in its own quiet way, it exposes the sickness at the heart of apartheid. It is less a play than a carefully choreographed series of variations upon the opening image: a naked man and woman, under a beam of light. Their bodies are the most eloquent testimony they can make of the destructive effects of the state upon their love. With *Orestes*, this is Fugard's most Grotowskian work, taking us further from social reality than before, but doing so to suggest the deep, instinctual dimensions of the relationship which the law seeks to disrupt.

There is an important sense in which it is precisely the point of this play to persuade us that 'statements' – about an event, a person, a relationship – distort, even destroy, what they describe. The 'statements' of the title are read out by a white policeman in a flat, unemotional voice, while the two lovers to whom they refer cower like trapped animals in the harsh glare of a torch. They are Frieda Joubert, the white librarian slipping into spinsterhood in a small Karroo town, and the 'Coloured' School principal, Errol Philander, who has been slinking out of the 'location', Bontrug, where his wife and children reside, at first to borrow books for his correspondence course, then to pursue a doubly illicit affair with the librarian.

Their relationship is in any case so very tentative, so riddled with guilt, that it is hard to believe in its survival even without the interference of the state. But Fugard wishes to suggest that the underlying impulse is stronger in the end than death. The defining image is a memory of two snakes, killed while copulating, whose bodies continue to move. This memory, one of the complex of images which was a 'mandate' for the play, comes to Philander (whose name could have been more subtly chosen) during the opening sequence, when he and his mistress, lying naked on the floor in post-coital tenderness, go over the events of the day. The snakes have been brought out into the open by the effect of the drought in his 'location'.

For Fugard, the whole country is in the grip of 'its worst drought', a drought 'in the human heart'; South Africa, he says, 'needs to be loved now, when it is at its ugliest',[6] a view it is hard to accept when we witness the ugliness shown in this play, the nightmare imposed upon the most secret, intimate moments by the intrusion of the state. The feeling of nightmare is strongest in the long middle sequence, in which camera flashes expose the man and woman tearing apart from an impulsive embrace, *'the man then scrambling for his trousers, finding them, and trying to put them on; the woman, naked, crawling around on the floor, looking for the man. As she finds him, and tries to hide behind his back, the flashes stop and torches are shone upon them. The torches are relentless, but we never see anything of the men behind them'.* The man then babbles in fright, trying to get into his trousers without exposing himself, but unsuccessfully; the woman shields him, turns to face the lights, and opens her mouth in a soundless scream like Munch's famous picture.

These are moments of sheer horror and, as played by Yvonne Bryceland and Ben Kingsley in the Royal Court production, they had an impact quite beyond the somewhat confused message of the work as a whole. Frozen by the unremitting glare, the two blurt out their 'statements': panic-stricken, guilty excuses, which become confessions, which become semi-poetic, fragmentary revelations of their lives. In pathetic contradiction of the simple, physical facts of their bodies, they accept the authoritarian logic which condemns them. The woman tries to explain that she was just helping the man with his studies, then admits her guilt, scrutinising her own body for its faults – the body she has feared even to show the man she loves in the safe light of a flickering match. 'I must be very still', she says, finally, isolated in a single light, 'because if I do anything, except think nothing, it will all start to happen, I won't be able to stop it.'

The clumsy, abstract feel of these words is, unfortunately, typical of the play. It is a weakness compounded by Philander's last speech about the loss of love – and himself. He too stands alone as he delivers it to us. But his alienation is more extreme than hers; it represents a culmination of all those emasculated men – Morris, Johnnie, Boesman – robbed of their ability to act, even to function at all. There are only 'my hands, and they are empty . . . there is only the emptiness left'. This 'statement' is bleakly pessimistic, touching ultimate despair. Without the humour that flickers intermittently in *Sizwe Bansi* and *The Island*, not to mention Fugard's earlier plays, *Statements* is a depressing work. Nevertheless, it is important, an example of an attempt to use theatre to suggest the primary drives – of libidinal and destructive energy – underlying social systems.

Fugard's determination to reach this level of implication is apparent in the tissue of allusions to evolution and the origins of life which he wove into the play after its early performances. Philander is obsessed with a phrase from Lyell's *Principles of Geology* (1832): 'no vestige of a beginning and no prospect of an end'. Life, Philander dimly realises, is a matter of endless suffering, as desire is defeated by death; but, somehow, absurdly, it continues. Fugard touches on a larger irony of history here, without being fully aware of it: Philander is himself the product of an evolutionary process which those who try to shape their own and others' destiny ignore – one of the truest South Africans, he is wholly evolved out of the contact between the races in the Cape, where they first met. The architects of apartheid seek to deny the people they themselves have brought into being: the 'Coloured' population is in every sense Afrikaans, yet is still denied by the Afrikaners (with the notable exception of a school of Afrikaans writers in the sixties, the *Sestigers*, who were condemned by Afrikanerdom in general).

Fugard himself sees *Statements after an Arrest* as the play which most nearly approaches his own views; and it is no coincidence that it is the most inward, since it is increasingly in the inner life of deeply instinctual drives that he locates the need for, if not the possibility of, change. He appears to be aware of the compromise inherent in this position.

Athol Fugard

Reflecting upon Ernst Fischer's description of the artist as 'commissioned by his society', Fugard asked himself,

> Do I want a commission? Have I got one? Must I function without one? Is my context as artist irremediably bourgeois? Can I align myself with a future, a possibility which I believe in (hope for) but of which I have no image? My failure of imagination?[7]

This is surprisingly, disarmingly honest. There *is* a failure of imagination, most evident when Fugard turns away from the creative energies he tapped in the production of *Sizwe Bansi* and *The Island*. But it is a failure of his class, his race, too: he is caught by the dilemma of his own position, a white liberal striving to proclaim the dignity of the human creature, but unable to anticipate how that dignity may be created, or participate in the movement which may create it.

Nevertheless, as we have seen, the most powerful moments in the *Statements* plays, their most memorable images, take us beyond the private pain in which his own concerns are rooted, to suggest the shape of suffering and hope for an entire community. It must not be forgotten that the creation of these plays coincided with the post-Sharpeville wave of repression which, amongst other things, silenced a generation, and ensured that barely any effective opposition to the omnipresent state could be expressed. Fugard survived: operating quietly in relatively low-risk ventures, but helping to bring about a significant contribution to radical, 'alternative' theatre, which extends way beyond the plays we have discussed here. 'Alternative' usually means simply fringe or experimental: drama created without the familiar hierarchy of writer, director, actor; drama performed without the familiar trappings of 'establishment' theatre. In this sense, all Fugard's work in the theatre may be called 'alternative', since, whatever the implications of subsequent success and assimiliation into the mainstream, it always begins as a low-cost, small-scale, makeshift if not improvised operation, in which he is simultaneously writer, director, and often, actor. This reflects his countinuing, obsessive concern with the 'pure theatre experience' conveyed by 'the actor and the stage, the actor *on* the stage'.

But, as a direct result of his contact with the Serpent Players and their township audiences, and indirectly as a result of the influence of Brecht and Grotowski, his conception of this experience was changed, so that, for a time at least, 'pure theatre' became, truly, 'poor theatre'. Such a theatre *is* capable of bearing witness.

6
Man Alone: 'Dimetos' and 'The Guest'

At the conclusion of *Dimetos* (1975), a man stands alone on the stage, laughing as he succeeds in juggling an imaginary object from hand to hand. 'And now, because your gaiety is so great,' he tells himself, 'the last skill of all. Hold them out, and wait . . . .' He extends his hands towards the audience, and waits. It is a strange, compelling and ambiguous gesture. What is he waiting for? The answer is suggested by the end of another, much greater play, *The Tempest*, with which *Dimetos* has a number of interesting parallels. As Shakespeare's play draws to its close, Prospero is left standing alone on the stage, his hands extended, as he addresses the audience with the words

> As you from crimes would pardon'd be
> Let your indulgence set me free.

Our clapping hands duly release him from the play's 'spell',
at the same time pardoning him. Prospero deserves redemption, as he deserves our applause: he has brought
things to a happy end by forgiving those who have
trespassed against him. The Christian overtones are un-
avoidable. But Dimetos has been unable to forgive, or be
forgiven. A 'guilty love' for his niece has led to her suicide,
and his madness; in a world without God, what hope can
there be of redemption? His hands are tainted, and so our
applause is reluctant, uncertain – assuming that we have
even understood that this is what his last gesture means.

The playwright came across the story of Dimetos in the
Carnets of Camus many years before, when it struck him as
the 'germinal idea' for a play; but it was not until a
commission from the Edinburgh International Festival
prompted a return to that 'appointment' that the play came
to be written. According to Camus's account, Dimetos had
a 'guilty love' for his niece, who hanged herself. One day a
beautiful, dead young woman was washed up by the sea.
Seeing her, Dimetos fell in love, but then had to watch the
decay of the body, an experience which drove him mad.
'This was his niece's vengeance', wrote Camus, 'and the
symbol of a condition which we must try to define'. Guilt,
and the forlorn hope of redemption, are at the heart of it.
Fugard's stage Dimetos is an engineer who has fled the city
because he no longer cares about its troubles. He becomes
aware of his secret passion when Lydia, his orphaned niece,
removes her dress in order to help rescue a horse fallen
down a well. Danilo, a young man from the city, arrives to
tempt Dimetos back. Dimetos vacillates, then uses the
unwitting emissary to arrange the near-rape of his niece. It
is Lydia's discovery that her uncle watched Danilo's
near-assault upon her from an adjoining lemon grove that
leads her to kill herself – using a rope knotted the way

Dimetos himself taught her. This concludes the first act. The second, many years later, finds Dimetos and his housekeeper Sophia (who is secretly in love with him) on a remote beach, where a sea creature crawls up on an offshore rock to die, and decay. Reduced to collecting shells for trading, Dimetos allows the smell of putrefaction to drive him insane. The only hint of hope emerges when the niece's spectral, off-stage voice offers him the chance to 'hold time' and come to grips with his own nature by turning it all into 'a story'. The artisan must become an artist. As Dimetos attempts this, beginning again at the beginning with 'Once upon a time, there was . . . a man . . . who dreamt he was a horse', his hands imitate those of a juggler who managed to 'give and take with the same action'. Then he holds his hands out, and waits . . . .

Dimetos's first audiences did not know what to make of the play – any more than they knew what to make of its immediate successor, *The Guest at Steenkampskraal* (1977), a film first shown on BBC TV two years after the premiere of *Dimetos*, but begun before the completion of *Dimetos* and then temporarily shelved for financial reasons. Fugard wrote the screenplay of *The Guest*, and put in a remarkable performance as its tormented hero, Eugène Marais. But it has since languished, largely ignored, if not forgotten. *Dimetos*'s fate has been worse. After 'private previews' in Cape Town, it became the first of Fugard's plays to be premiered outside his native country when it appeared at the Church Hill Theatre, Edinburgh, as part of the 1975 International Festival. Poor acoustics, uncertain direction and the inexperience of the Afrikaans newcomer brought over to play the lead exacerbated the difficulties of the text to provoke widespread disappointment and denunciation. Fugard reworked and revived the play the following year at the Nottingham

Playhouse and then in London's West End with Paul Scofield in the lead; but not even a clearer script and Scofield's presence could overcome the continuing problems *Dimetos* posed. Above all, as its most enthusiastic supporter at the time, Ned Chaillet, pointed out in *Plays and Players*, it was *Dimetos*'s 'unexpected non-political nature' which caused dismay and confusion, and no amount of tinkering with text of staging or cast could alter that. Unlike the preceding *Statements* plays – still fresh in everyone's minds – *Dimetos* departed from explicitness and the daily experiences of the victims of apartheid to explore the inner doubt and self-questioning of a white man among whites, in a remote and timeless setting. *The Guest* at least dealt with a specific, historically recognisable incident in a known setting – the Heidelberg district of the Transvaal in 1926, when the poet–naturalist Marais attempted to cure himself of morphine addiction. But this also seemed to represent a withdrawal from the current realities of South Africa – which was then in the midst of the Soweto riots.

The fiercest criticism made of Fugard during this time came from within the burgeoning Black Consciousness movement in South Africa, the attempted suppression of which sparked off the uprising of June 1976. Fatima Meer, a leader of the Black Women's Federation who had been detained without trial, wrote to Fugard from prison to ask how, after *Sizwe Bansi* and *The Island*, he could involve himself in work so 'totally without political commitment and therefore valueless in terms of the urgent and violent realities of our time'. 'What can I say in reply?' he asked himself. When *Dimetos* first appeared, he had admitted being 'finished as a committed political writer'; that play was 'a profound personal statement using inner specifics in defining the condition of modern man'. But perhaps this was the point. Writing was in itself a 'form of action'.

Telling 'a story', even if only of 'one man's hell', retained significance, which was the significance of a 'long-term investment', unlike the acknowledged but only immediate returns of, say, political pamphlets.[1] The key to what might redeem Dimetos turns out to be an attempt to tell 'a story', *his* story, shortly before the end of the play; which, in so far as it is convincing, suggests Fugard's real answer to the attack on his work. His 'commitment' has always been to his own 'complex of images', which he hopes 'bear witness' to the sufferings of others, to a struggle not his own, rather than to any direct political statement. Exploring his own despair, he has tried to explore that of his countrymen as well.

Dimetos and *The Guest* are, however, undeniably further from the social and political realities of his time than their predecessors. They are also, in their own way, revealing and symptomatic. Nadine Gordimer's *July's People* (1981), a novel about a group of whites trying to survive in the rural retreat to which they have escaped from the city, in which the revolution has at last broken out, opens with an epigraph from Gramsci's *Prison Notebooks*: 'The old is dying and the new cannot be born; in this interregnum there arises a great diversity of morbid symptoms.' It is no coincidence that, when *Dimetos* and *The Guest* appeared, other white liberal writers were veering away from direct treatment of the crises then facing their country towards symbolic, unspecific modes of storytelling – a trend most obvious in the novels of J. M. Coetzee, like Fugard a half-Afrikaner who writes in English. The impotence of white dissidents to effect change in the face of the rising generation of politically conscious blacks is expressed in terms of a retreat into self-scrutiny, fantasy, and an obsession with the psychopathology of the isolated consciousness.

In Fugard, this appears as a reaction to the collaborative phase of his career, a turning-inwards, into being 'very private with myself and a blank paper' after having, as he put it, allowed his 'life and energies' to be 'hijacked' by others. Dimetos expresses his creator's feelings when he remarks, 'I'm tired of other men's needs, other men's disasters.' This coincides with a new emphasis in *Dimetos* and *The Guest* upon 'man alone . . . there are other people, but the predicament is being alone'.[2] Both works focus upon one central figure; the other characters function as so many different, fragmentary perspectives upon this man's anguished preoccupation with himself and the meaning of his life. Inevitably, Dimetos and Marais evoke limited sympathy: martyrs to their own cause, they are unable to accept succour, much less offer it. Both men are artists of a kind, evidently alter egos for the playwright, struggling to come to terms with his own position.

Dimetos, then, is a meditation upon guilt, and the role of the artist in a situation inducing guilt. The problem is that Fugard tries to universalise this before he has begun to relate it to where it belongs. When he was revising *Dimetos* after its disastrous premiere, he found himself changing the 'remote province' of Act I to New Bethesda, a small Karroo village to which he escapes from Port Elizabeth; Act II was transformed from 'beside the ocean' to Gaukamma Beach, a desolate spot familiar to him. But he has resisted any further particularising of the story, preferring to believe that as it stands it will eventually find its audience – a belief that has so far had little confirmation. Instead, he has himself turned back towards the local detail and accent of his earlier 'Port Elizabeth' plays, with considerable success.

The vagueness and uncertainty which beset *Dimetos* are present from the start, which is marked by what must rank as one of the more extraordinary opening stage directions in the theatre today: '*Lydia is lowered to the bottom of a well to tie ropes round a horse that has fallen down it.*' In the early productions, Fugard directed that this should be managed on a stage empty apart from a bench and a rope – a rope which the actor playing Dimetos has then to throw down to a half-naked young actress standing a few feet away in the dim light, where she pretends she is astride a desperate horse down a well. She has to carry out instructions bellowed 'down' to her by her uncle, tying imaginary slings around the terrified beast so that it may be safely pulled back to the surface. One ingenious solution, adopted by a recent (1981) production at the People's Space in Cape Town, was to isolate Dimetos and the girl in single overhead spots, the latter crouching upon a raised platform within a gauze tube suspended from the rafters to suggest the well, while ropes working through overhead pulleys connected uncle and niece in their joint struggle to free the 'horse'. The sensuality of this opening image is essential – the girl twisting about as she straddles the heaving body of the horse – since we must feel Dimetos's vain effort to resist the desire welling up within himself later when Lydia emerges and innocently dries herself with her dress. But it is hard not to be distracted by the sheer mechanics of the scene, to miss what it is all supposed to represent – mainly, it seems, the law of gravity, and its usefulness to Dimetos's strong hands.

Dimetos's hands are repeatedly referred to as if they were separable from the man himself, and in some way an expression of his inner being: first tying knots, then rubbing his niece's back dry, and then, towards the climax of the first act, giving up the tell-tale smell of crushed lemons; in the second act, his hands are said to have 'come to an end', as we discover him '*fiddling compulsively*' with beach debris. Even when he goes on to set his hands to work again, arranging stones and shells into a kind of order on his workbench, this proves 'useless'. Like earlier characters in Fugard's plays, he is searching for a truth (in Camus's words in *The Myth of Sisyphus*) that his 'hands can touch'; but can he find it? This dramatic motif has been anticipated by the moment in *Boesman and Lena* when Lena says to her bullying partner, 'Open your fist, put your hand on me . . . .' But Boesman cannot; he strikes her instead. Yet Lena at least has something to offer, when she opens her hands. At the end of *Statements after an Arrest under the Immorality Act*, Philander stands alone on the darkened stage with 'nothing left, just my hands, and they are empty'.

The laws of physics are what Dimetos the engineer knows and believes in. But, as the first act demonstrates by rescue of the horse and the girl's suicide, an understanding of these laws can destroy as well as save – a fact of experience which totally undermines Dimetos, as it undermines his sense of the universe as logically ordered according to scientific and technological knowledge. What he awaits at the end, it seems, is that revelation which will keep us 'From Single vision & Newton's sleep!', in the words of the play's epigraph. Like Dimetos, Fugard waits for the inspiration which might clarify it all. The playwright will have received more hindrance than help from the book which most impressed him at the time as confirming the direction in which he was attempting to go – Theodore Roszak's *Where the Wasteland Ends* (1972), a vague, rambling and unoriginal account of how the scientific revolution and its aftermath have alienated us from ourselves and the universe. According to Roszak, it is by reaching always for 'hard fact' that we leave ourselves 'empty-handed', when we should be like St Francis, our hands 'open to the birds, empty, yet full'. But Dimetos's hands are not those of a saint. How could they be?

If we are moved by Dimetos's plight – mainly during the second act, when his world has cracked open under the strain of trying to ignore his pervasive sense of guilt – it is difficult to feel his strength, or to imagine him as having the stature Fugard evidently wishes to suggest. Without that faith in himself or others – much less in God – which might conceivably lead to his redemption, his empty-handed final gesture is pathetic, rather than profound or tragic. He is, ultimately, a small man, persuaded by the blind love of those closest to him, as well as the adulation of those more distant, that his plight is universal, when it is his own, and self-created. He is a white South African, not a mythical Greek; indeed, an Afrikaner. And his form of romanticism is characteristic of the Afrikaner, attempting to escape the burden of the present by indulging in fantasies about a pre-industrial, 'tribal' society in which the 'traditional' (i.e. feudal) order ensures harmony and security. It is to Fugard's credit that, while he exhibits a yearning for this ideal, he also realises it is a kind of madness, the product of his people's deep guilt.

This painful truth is closer to the surface in *The Guest*, in which Fugard continues to try to take stock of his position as 'man alone', and generalise it, but this time by means of a version of an incident in the life of the Afrikaner culture hero Marais, with whom he identifies himself as he identified with Dimetos. For Fugard, long an admirer of both Marais's poetry and his studies of nature, the small episode at Steenkampskraal with which the film deals contains in essence the story of the man's life, which is revealed in the magisterial Afrikaans biography by Leon Rousseau, *Die Groot Verlange* (1974), the main source of Fugard's script. A brief outline may suggest why Fugard was attracted to Marais. Eugène Marais was born in 1871, in Pretoria, the thirteenth child of a 'genteelly poor'

Afrikaner family from the Cape. His invalid father was bankrupted by the Anglo-Boer War of 1881; thereafter he was brought up by his siblings. The family spoke English at home, and considered themselves superior to up-country Afrikaners who spoke the local Dutch-derived dialect. Marais always found English easier to speak and write than Afrikaans, and he was steeped in English literature. Yet the little poetry he did write was in Afrikaans, contributing a handful of verses which confirmed the potential of what was then still only a dialect. At first a journalist in his home town, Marais went on to study law in London during the 1890s, an experience which ensured that he became less and less like the typical Afrikaner. Widely read, 'cultured', 'decadent', and a freethinker interested in the workings of the sub-conscious mind, he developed profoundly ambivalent feelings towards his own people – like Fugard after him. By 1907 he had retreated to the remote Waterberg area of the Transvaal in the first of a long series of attempts to seek solace for his secret addiction to morphine. He had always looked to nature for some explanation of his own suffering; and in the Waterberg he observed a troop of chacma baboons whose behaviour seemed to offer an answer. In a passage repeated in Fugard's film, Marais noted how silence fell upon the troop with the first deepening of the shadows at sunset, the older members assuming

> attitudes of profound dejection. It is hardly possible to avoid the conclusion that the chacma suffers from the same attribute of pain which is such an important ingredient of human mentality, and that the condition is due to the same cause, namely, the suffering inseparable from the new mind which like man the chacma has acquired in the course of its evolution.

No scientist, Marais nevertheless produced two remarkable accounts of his observations and meditations: *The Soul of the Ape*, which he never finished, but which was finally published in 1969 with an enthusiastic introduction by Robert Ardrey; and *The Soul of the White Ant* (1935), which proposed that the white-ant or termite nest was a single organism, an idea widely supposed in South Africa to have been plagiarised by the Nobel Prizewinner Maurice Maeterlinck. Despite the celebrity this brought Marais, his life had long become fixed in a downward spiral of failed attempts to overcome his addiction, and on 25 July 1936 he shot himself.

'You will look in vain in nature for love, sympathy, pity, justice ... from the very beginnings of life, we hear a chorus of anguish. Pain is a condition of existence.' Marais's dark vision runs like an irresistible current through *The Guest*, surfacing most effectively in the form of disturbing, dream-like images derived from memories of his time with the chacma baboons of the Waterberg, images accompanied by voice-over quotations like this from *The Soul of the Ape*. Marais is depicted as almost entirely lost within his own, intensely inward thought processes, unresponsive to others except briefly when he appears to find the path to recovery, only to relapse again at the end. The overall tone of the film is that of unsparing documentary: shot in black and white, lucid, unsentimental, bare and brief, it represents a triumph for director Ross Devenish, whose main previous experience was limited to television reportage (apart from the first collaboration with Fugard on the film version of *Boesman and Lena*, little more than a filmed play).

The Guest opens as it closes, with a car in long-shot being driven across the bare, scorched veld. Marais (Fugard) is being taken by his friend and fellow poet, Dr Visser

(Marius Weyers), to Steenkampskraal, where his latest, long-overdue 'cure' will begin. He sits sunk in drug-induced, numb unconcern. Invariably 'the guest' of those who can be persuaded to put up with him for a time, his struggle to come to some kind of equilibrium once again is to take place in a setting where humanity only survives on tolerance – the tolerance of nature. Oom ('Uncle') Doors Meyer and his wife Tant ('Aunt') Corrie, their two grown-up farmer sons Doorsie and Louis and small daughter Little Corrie know nothing of literature, science or drugs, but they have come to a temporary accommodation with their environment, and can offer a home, family and sustenance. A large-boned, slow-moving and (at first) patient group, they are transformed by the impact of Marais's presence into a state of uncertainty and disorientation, in which they can do little but rely on the Calvinist faith represented by the great family Bible. Their genuine hospitality is soon disrupted as Marais lies sweating and screaming in bed while they try to say grace and eat their meals; the two young men with whom he shares a cell-like room soon discover he is injecting himself secretly; and, when he appears to recover, and goes out into the farmland with them, it is to dissect a termite nest – an act which offends their sense of the divinity of nature. But Marais's recovery is short-lived, and the inevitable relapse follows, as he descends into near-madness yelling, 'Desdemona lives again, black man!' in a voice which drowns out that of Oom Doors, trying to read out aloud to his family from their Dutch Bible. In the closing sequence, the car takes Marais away along the same road: nothing has been resolved, we end where we began, and the traditional, rural, God-fearing Afrikaners have only provided an illusion of security.

The pessimistic tone of the film is confirmed by the

repetition of the opening shots at the end; yet something has been suggested of the survival of the creative urge in an environment of endless, incomprehensible suffering – the urge to articulate the meaning of that suffering, at least. Marais's closest relationship in his declining years was with a five-year-old girl, on whom he lavished his lasting gift: story-telling. As in *Dimetos*, Fugard focuses on this as a redemptive possibility, and in a central, touching sequence of the film we see Marais noticing Little Corrie's fantasy world of fairies, going on to carve a stick with which he prints a series of miniature footprints leading to the cellar where she believes they live, and then relating to her his poem 'Die Spinerak-rokkie' – the story of a fairy dress of cobwebs which is no sooner put on than the wind sweeps it away. Perilously close to sentimentality at this point, Devenish's deft economy of style keeps the film to its main subject: the fragility of the creative spirit. Marais lacks the resilience which Tant Corrie's suffering has inspired in her – she tells him of her time in a British concentration camp during the Anglo-Boer War; but she lacks the complex self-awareness, the insight, which his experiences have brought him.

Marais's art survives, it seems. As the camera pans across the bleak veld in the last shot, away from the lonely figure of the man, we hear his most famous poem, 'Die Lied van Suid-Afrika' ('The Song of South Africa'), a 'song' which sums up, for Fugard, the meaning of the film, and its 'relevance'. South Africa, a female voice, speaks about herself and her people: she has thrown them from the mountains, smothered them in the deserts, allowed them to hunger and thirst; tears and lamentations, gestures of supplication, are of no avail; giving nothing, she demands everything. It is her holy right. The trouble with this view is that it prompts the question, is this endless suffering really a precondition of existence, or more specifically a precondition of the Afrikaner's existence in South Africa? Further, what do the whites whose 'story' (rather than history) this is know of the suffering of that vast, ignored continent of people represented in *The Guest* by 'Stuurie', the African farmworker whose sole task appears to be the provision of Marais's drugs from the distant town, and whose only words are, significantly, *'Ja, baas'*? On some level, the film suggests, the African is 'present' to Marais: in his 'madness', it is a vision of *Othello* which swims before his eyes. But what does that mean? If anything, the parallel seems to be between himself and Iago, another disrupter of relationships, of hope. Perhaps, again, like Dimetos, Marais is intended to be awaiting redemption: 'I can thy former light restore if I repent me', he exclaims as he stares out into the night; but he too lacks any saving grace.

All Fugard's works carry a penumbra of sub-textual suggestiveness, realisable only in production; but production failed to illuminate the obscurities of *Dimetos* and *The Guest*. Nevertheless, both works constitute a remarkable attempt to respond to inner promptings to embark upon a quest of self-discovery. And, although this involved the playwright in a return to more conventional methods of working, it also took him into new areas of expression, the mixed genres of symbolic drama and film. If *Dimetos* is flawed, it is by no means impossible to stage; and *The Guest*, which has suffered by being conveyed in the narrower medium of television, with its in-built tendency towards naturalism, would be more effective distributed in cinema, where a wider range of expectations is available. Fugard's own valuation of both works (especially *Dimetos*) remains high; perhaps they were a necessary stage in his development.

7
Port Elizabeth Revisited: 'Marigolds', 'Aloes' and ' "Master Harold" . . . and the boys'

As if to compensate for the vagueness and obscurity of *Dimetos* and, to a lesser extent, *The Guest*, Fugard's succeeding works have been almost excessively clear, even didactic. This has coincided with a return to the familiar setting, textures and accent of his home environment – to the 'specifics' of Port Elizabeth, expressed in a form of naturalism not restricted to the evocation of locale, but shot through with explicit, metaphoric 'lessons' – for example in the very title of *A Lesson from Aloes* (1978). As Sam, one of the 'boys' in *'Master Harold' . . . and the boys* (1982), puts it, there has been 'a hell of a lot of teaching going on'. This carries with it a danger which Fugard himself recognises:

I strive quite consciously and deliberately for ambiguity of expression because it is superior to singleness of meaning and reflects the nature of life . . . [but] . . . my whole temperament inclines me to be very unequivocal indeed. That is not difficult – but it would be at the cost of truth.[1]

The cost is evident in *Marigolds in August*, a film begun on completion of *The Guest*, but not finished until three years later, in 1979. In it, two black men, Daan and Melton, are shown struggling to survive in the all-white coastal resort of Schoenmakerskop, near Port Elizabeth, the Fugards' home at the time. They are brought to understand their position by a wise old 'Coloured' snake-catcher, Paulus, played by Fugard with a laboured sagacity which makes all too obvious his conception of himself as their mediator and teacher. *Marigolds*, which won a clutch of South African Oscars, is ostensibly about the difficulties faced by black people in a society which forces them into 'unnatural' situations in order to survive – like the marigolds which Daan, a gardener and odd-job man, is made to plant in August, a winter month in South Africa. Daan (Winston Ntshona) thinks his meagre living is threatened by the arrival of the younger, unemployed Melton (John Kani), desperate because of his starving family. But, as Paulus explains, the two are subject to the same dilemma: how to survive under the domination of the whites – a pervasive, but scarcely seen presence in the film.

Marigolds may be understood as the final part of a trilogy with the other Fugard–Devenish collaborations: the *Boesman and Lena* film, which focused on the struggle to survive of a 'Coloured' couple; *The Guest*, in which it was the turn of the Afrikaner; and now, the African. But, as Fugard departs from the experience most familiar to him, or most accessible, the limitations of his approach become correspondingly more apparent. In the absence of his close knowledge and observation of 'Coloured' vagrants or isolated Afrikaners, and without the opportunities provided earlier by collaboration with the Sophiatown group or Serpent Players, he adopts the role of the white man without whom, it seems, Africans are unable to understand the implications of their own situation. The black actors in *Marigolds* were, in fact, members of the defunct Serpent Players; without the relative independence formerly possible, however, their participation was restricted. The difficulties involved in the creation of the film are exemplified by what happened when Fugard met the original of Melton: unable to speak the man's language (Xhosa), the playwright noted the 'abysmal lack of communication between us'; yet he went on to assume from the man's demeanour as he talked to their translator and go-between, John Kani, that 'All he wants to do is live his life.'[2] Though Kani invested his performance of Melton with an understanding which occasionally persuades us of its authenticity, the impression remains that Fugard has predetermined the relationship between the two black men and its outcome so as to suit his 'lesson'.

Given the playwright's earlier success in helping to articulate the 'township' experience, it is understandable that he should think of himself as a voice, a mediator. But times have changed, and so has his position. Not only is he more isolated nowadays, in terms of contact with local black people not either servants or chance acquaintances; but black people increasingly wish to speak in their own voice. As the late Steve Biko complained more than ten years ago, not only have the whites 'kicked the black but they have also told him how to react to that kick'.[3] Impatience with white liberals is longstanding, and widespread. Yet *Marigolds* is not *entirely* compromised by white liberal unawareness. Fugard and Devenish's responsiveness to the potential of the telling image, the visual, dramatic 'moment', does on occasion take the film beyond itself. The best example is a sequence towards the end, which shows Melton alone in the deserted bungalow of a white family, whose personal mementoes seem to mock the need which has driven him to break into their house; with an angry, futile gesture, the young black man sweeps all their photographs, knick-knacks and so on onto the floor, and departs.

The message is clear, and it underlies the overt 'lessons' of both *Aloes* and *'Master Harold'*: violence and destruction are inevitable, unless the whites see and respond to the demands of their submerged, suffering population. In *Aloes*, that population is invisible, but the inability of the characters to respond to any but their own needs renders them impotent, defeated; in *'Master Harold'*, the young white boy at the centre of the play is faced with the choice of joining with the blacks in brotherhood, or remaining 'master', in isolation and impending darkness. Both plays are retrospective in manner as well as matter; the disturbing pressures of the moment nevertheless make themselves felt. Brotherhood, and its obverse, betrayal, are recurrent themes in these plays, written at a time when the appalling human consequences of South Africa's growing, irresistible, undeclared war are becoming frighteningly obvious. As far as Fugard is concerned, survival remains the basic, crippling demand: crippling because of its cost, which, he now realises, may involve isolation, madness or exile.

These possibilities are present in *A Lesson from Aloes*, in what happens to its three characters – the middle-aged Afrikaner Piet Bezuidenhout, once 'politicised' but now left alone in his stubborn determination to stick everything out; his English-speaking wife, Gladys, who has experienced the 'rape' of her private, female world by the security police – an experience which has driven her to insanity, and will again; and Steve Daniels, their 'Coloured' activist friend, who finally chooses an 'exit permit' and exile in preference to banning and imprisonment. The action of the play is simple, and is designed to reveal each character's past experiences, and the present result. It centres on a farewell dinner the Bezuidenhouts have set up for Steve and his family. Everything takes place over a few hours late one afternoon and evening, shifting from the backyard of Xanadu, the Bezuidenhouts' home, to their bedroom inside, and back again. The staging, which is the same throughout, physically separates Piet's and Gladys's exterior, 'social' world, the world in which they will meet Steve, from the bedroom which functions as Gladys's private, intimate realm, and where she keeps her personal diary. The first act reveals Piet and Gladys in conversation prior to Steve's arrival; the second, what transpires as a result of his arrival, and departure. The pivot of the action is the discovery that Piet is believed to have informed on his comrades in the (unspecified) liberation movement, and in particular upon Steve, who broke his 'banning order' to attend a party, after which he was captured by the police, interrogated and imprisoned for six months. By the end of the play it is clear Piet has been unjustly suspected. But in the course of the evening we have learnt how all three feel they have been betrayed in one way or another – an experience which has destroyed their faith in each other, if not in themselves. Piet alone retains faith in himself, although it is hard to understand why.

Fugard has called *A Lesson from Aloes* a 'celebration' of the Afrikaner; it is dedicated to his mother; and in the introduction to the published edition he appears to identify with his stubborn, big-hearted Afrikaner hero, who loves literature and who is opposed to the defeatism of others. Piet has, as Gladys puts it, a 'gross certainty in himself', offensive to her as it is to their friend Steve, since it is out of their reach; and its very existence implies they lack an equivalent moral strength. Despite this, Piet's hopes and regrets, his desires and ideals, can be touching – for us, if not for them. When the play opens, Piet is seated in the backyard of Xanadu, surrounded by a collection of aloes in a variety of tins, with a 'newcomer' in his hand that he is trying to identify. 'Names are more than just labels', he informs Gladys, who sits very still on a garden bench nearby, her expression hidden by a pair of large sunglasses. His 'face', his 'story' are in his name, as much as Romeo's and Juliet's were in theirs: 'Then deny thy father and refuse thy name', Piet quotes; 'Hell! I don't know about those Italians, but that's a hard one for an Afrikaner.' We laugh, but there is a serious point: Piet's identity is inextricably tied up with his background, his 'story' – which is, like that of Gladys and Steve, a story of suffering. Like them, Piet is offered his chance to tell his story, and he does. Initially, it is a familiar tale – familiar, that is, to anyone who has lived in Africa. He tells of being forced off the land by drought. But the details define a specific, personal sense of shame, and failure:

> PIET. ... One of the last little chores of Baas Bezuidenhout on the farm was to put on his black suit and join an African family that had worked for him – and his father before him – around a little grave out in the veld. A baby had died. Gastroenteritis. There hadn't been a drop of clean water on Alwynlaagte ... the farm ... for God alone knows how many months. They hadn't 'dug' that hole, Steve. They'd used a pick and crowbars to break into the ground, it was so dry. Anyway ... when it came to my turn to say a few

words . . . (*Piet shakes his head*). That hole with the little homemade coffin defeated me . . . .

His subsequent involvement with the 'Coloured' people's bus boycott seemed to bring 'rain after a long drought'; but that, too, ended in defeat. As Steve points out, the reason for defeat lies not in nature but in their own inadequacies: 'We were like a bunch of boy scouts playing at politics. Those boer-boys play the game rough. It's going to need men who don't care about the rules to sort them out. That was never us.' This much Steve has learnt from *his* defining, painful experience – as he is prompted to confess when Piet refuses to deny or admit he was responsible for his friend's arrest: he laughs;

> I'm sorry, Piet, but I mean it. That's very, very funny. I think those were my exact words when they started questioning me after the party. They made a few jokes in the car, but I kept quiet . . . you see, hiding there in Betty's wardrobe while they searched the place . . . squashed in the dark there among her clothes . . . with her perfume and me shit-scared . . . it came up, man. Hard! I was trying to hit the damned thing down when they found me. And they saw it. In the car one of them said: 'If you don't teach it to behave, Daniels, we'll take it away from you.' I was scared, Piet. I knew where I was going. Anyway, up there on the fifth floor the questions really started . . . .

Like Morris, Johnnie, Boesman and Philander before him, Daniels feels his manhood threatened by the workings of the apartheid state; not surprisingly, he breaks under interrogation, and tells all he knows. But the final humiliation is yet to come: when he has finished his statement, his interrogators pat him on the back, and say, 'Well done, Daniels! But now tell us something we don't know.'

Betrayal has destroyed Steve Daniels, and there is nothing left for him but to leave the country. This option is not open to Gladys, who is tied by her relationship to Piet – although, as Steve points out, 'If I had a white skin, I'd also find lots of reasons for not leaving this country.' For Gladys, 'politics' and 'the black man's misery' are meaningless; yet it is precisely the pressure of politics and black misery which led to the security-police raid on their home, and the removal of her intimate diaries. She is trapped in the contradictions of her position. Born in South Africa, she denies it is her home; but she is unable to leave, with the result that she ends up in 'Fort England' (a mental hospital in Grahamstown). 'I accept, Steven,' she tells Daniels, 'that I am just a white face on the outskirts of your terrible life, but I'm in the middle of mine and yours is just a brown face on the outskirts of that. Do you understand what I'm saying? I've got my own story. I don't need yours. I've discovered hell for myself.' The end of the play suggests that little more can be said. Steve departs, she prepares to return to the hospital, and Piet sits in the backyard, puzzling over his unidentified aloe.

A Lesson from Aloes is not a political play, although its characters talk about, and have been deeply affected by, politics. The key speech, summing up what the playwright wishes us to take from it, is uttered by Piet, when he tells his wife the 'lesson' he learnt from Steve when they first met: 'An evil system', he says, 'isn't a natural disaster. There's nothing you can do to stop a drought, but bad laws and social injustice are man-made and can be unmade by men. It's as simple as that.' If we are to take these words seriously, then nothing could be worse than Piet's inactivity, left sitting contemplating his aloes. Fugard apparently cannot see this. Brecht, too, observed in *The Messingkauf Dialogues* that 'Nothing human can possibly lie outside the powers of humanity'; but he understood that group conflicts cannot be overcome by individual action alone. When Fugard tries to suggest the wider meaning of the situation in which his characters are trapped, he becomes contradictory, or at least confused. The aloe, a tenacious, indigenous plant which thrusts its thorny leaves and flame-like spears of flowers through the most barren Eastern Cape soil, might seem an irresistible emblem for survival. But what we are left with at the end of *A Lesson from Aloes* is hopeless passivity and retreat. Most reviewers outside South Africa found the play unconvincing for this reason. One notable exception, however, was James Fenton, who saw the production during a successful London season at the Cottesloe Theatre in 1980: he found that Fugard's 'great strength in this work derives from an intimate knowledge of defeat and the consequences of defeat . . . those who really know what defeat is are in a better position to lead their companions to victory'.[4]

This is arguable, but it does suggest how *Aloes* may be most effectively understood and presented: in terms of the historical reality of its setting, which is remarkably precise. *Aloes* is set, as Piet is made to announce early on, in Algoa Park, Port Elizabeth, in 1963 – that is, in the lower middle class, predominantly Afrikaans suburb adjoining the 'ugly Coloured area with all the factories', i.e. Cadles, through which Piet takes a bus on the run through the boycott which politicised him. That boycott preceded Steve's first visit to Xanadu, a visit which coincided with the birth of his son, Little Pietertjie, almost seven years before the time of the play. This locates the bus boycott as one of many such acts of small-scale resistance to the authorities during the late fifties: significant enough to those who, like Steve and Piet, participated in them, but overshadowed by the events which followed, and which created the mood of defeat which pervades the play. In July 1963, the major resistance movements, which had been forced underground in the aftermath of Sharpeville, seemed to face extinction when an informer led police to the farm in Rivonia, near Johannesburg, which proved to be the hideout of their High Command. Mass trials on charges of sabotage and treason ended in imprisonment for life of the leaders, including Nelson Mandela. The impact upon the Eastern Cape, including members of the Serpent Players, has already been described. But there were others Fugard knew who were affected; and the man upon whom Piet Bezuidenhout is modelled he met as far back as 1961, when the main ideas and images of *A Lesson from Aloes* first came to him. The play takes us back into the past, and its mood of paralysis reflects an inability to face the present, or contemplate the future. In this respect, it touches on the current situation of the impotent white liberal with penetrating accuracy – a situation driving Fugard yet further into his own past, as his next play revealed.

'Master Harold' . . . and the boys is dated 1950, and is Fugard's most directly autobiographical work. It continues the didactic naturalism of *Marigolds* and *Aloes* but, mercifully, without their somewhat forced horticultural symbolism; instead, a pattern of images is adopted which is more integral to the characters and their situation, and which operates with more dramatic impact. The whole play, which runs without an interval the realistic hundred minutes of its action, builds to a climax as shocking as it is unexpected, the 'living moment' and defining image of the work: the teenage white boy at its centre spits in the face of one of his mother's black servants. It is one of the theatre's most disturbing moments; and it should be no surprise to

realise that it has taken Fugard almost his whole career so far to be able to disclose the incident from which his deepest feelings of guilt and remorse derive. For many years he has carried the memory of that act of adolescent betrayal, unable to talk about or deal with it; for years, too, he has felt a need to 'celebrate' Sam Semela, the Basuto waiter who was his only 'significant' friend as a white schoolboy in Port Elizabeth. Finally, about a year before the premiere of '*Master Harold*' at the Yale Repertory Theatre in New Haven in 1982, he came to realise that an image of the two black servants, Sam and Willy, which had been revolving in his mind as the idea for a play, had to be seen in relation to a white boy – himself. He had, finally, arrived at that 'moment which totally symbolised the ugliness, the potential ugliness waiting for me as a white South African', an experience of his own and his country's racialism. 'The play is an attempt to share that experience with the audience.'[5]

As audiences all over the world agreed, he succeeded. The climactic moment of '*Master Harold*' aroused in spectators everywhere a painful, shared awareness of the personal roots of racialism, of the secret ugliness we all harbour within ourselves in our most intimate relation-ships, and which provides the motive force for some of the worst excesses of our time, in the outbursts of hatred and violence with which we are all too familiar. The exorcism of Fugard's private guilt has provided an opportunity for the exorcism of a public guilt. Like all his plays, '*Master Harold*' is primarily about relationships, although it has its broader social and political implications; but in its short, concentrated structure it develops a more intensely moving effect than perhaps any of its predecessors, with the result that it is not easy to understand clearly what it is saying. But this takes us back to the basic point about his work: it is his greatest strength as a dramatist to move us deeply by his account of the South African experience; it is his greatest weakness that he is unable to analyse that experience, or be clear about its social and historical implications. The ambiguity of his images allows us to recognise a radical, cutting edge to his work, just as we have to admit a tendency to reflect the status quo. Our response is further complicated by Fugard's recent homiletic urge, apparent once again in the somewhat heavy-handed explication of 'lessons'.

The events of *'Master Harold'* are deceptively simple; and they are played out against a setting – the remembered home of Fugard's teenage years when his mother ran the St George's Park Tearoom in the centre of Port Elizabeth – more detailedly realistic than before. A serving-counter with a cash register and a few stale cakes under glass on one side of the tearoom is balanced by an old jukebox on the other, the space between linked upstage by a window looking out onto a windy, wet afternoon. A few sad ferns sit in pots on the window ledge, before which a number of tables and chairs are stacked. Downstage there stands a small table and chair; on the table, a knife, fork, spoon and side plate, together with a pile of comics, anticipate the simple meal that has been prepared for the returning schoolboy, 'Master Harold'. A chalkboard menu, advertisements for Coca-Cola and other beverages, a telephone, wastebin and the other small appurtenances of a tearoom complete this picture from the past. There is an exit to the kitchen at one side behind the counter; and an entrance from the park through a glass door to the tearoom on the other.

The two black men present as the play begins seem to take inordinate pride in these shabby surroundings: Willie, sleeves and trousers rolled up, is painstakingly mopping down the floor with a bucket of water and a rag, kneeling carefully on a folded piece of cardboard, his apron tucked between his legs; Sam, wearing the brass-buttoned white jacket, white shirt, black bow tie and trousers of a waiter, leans nonchalantly on the solitary table, paging idly through a comic book. Willie is singing while he works. He gets up, and swings heavily into a dance step with an imaginary partner. This leads to a discussion of the forthcoming New Brighton Ballroom Dancing Competition. Sam instructs Willie how to avoid mistakes. Like Styles and Robert/Sizwe before them, the men immediately strike us as a contrasting pair: Willie is as awkward as Sam is graceful, and he has to listen as Sam offers guidance to him on the quickstep and his partner, the unseen Hilda. It must look like 'romance', Sam tells Willie; 'when the judges look at you and Hilda, they must see a man and a woman who are dancing their way to a happy ending. What I saw was you holding her like you were frightened she was going to run away'. '*Ja!*' replies Willie. 'Because that is what she wants to do!'

The gap between the impossible, ideal world imagined by Sam and the harsh, even violent reality known to Willie, gently and humorously anticipates the main theme of the play. The terrible loneliness brought about by the betrayal at its centre is offset by the idea of dancing as a paradigm of universal harmony. Sadly, that harmony seems as far out of reach as the kite which Sam once made for 'Hally' – as he affectionately calls the white schoolboy whose arrival interrupts the conversation between the two men, obliging Willie to return to the floor, and Sam to the kitchen, from which he brings Hally's lunch. 'Master Harold', as Willie respectfully addresses him, starts to talk about his schoolwork and, uninterrupted by customers as the rain patters continuously down outside, the three spend the rest of the afternoon and the play following the threads of shared memory, alternately bantering and serious, that this uncovers – jarred only by telephone calls from the hospital, where Hally's father is being treated for his amputated leg. These calls provoke the frustrated, unhappy outbursts which culminate in Hally's abuse of Sam – his surrogate father. The white boy's adolescent naïvety and dogmatism are finely caught, as is his patronising affection for his mentor. 'There's something called progress', he informs Sam, when the servants tell of the beatings black men receive in prison, an account vividly mimed by Sam and Willie. Hally's idea of progress is as limited as his idea of history: 'You've never been a slave, you know', he tells Sam; 'And anyway we freed your ancestors here in South Africa long before the Americans.'

All three evidently enjoy these exchanges, which take them back to the Jubilee Boarding house servants' quarters, where Hally first met Sam and Willie, and which they recall by re-enacting a scene together, according to Hally's 'stage directions'. Then, just as the two men and the boy seem closest, the present reasserts itself in the first telephone call from Hally's mother. The prospect of his father returning from hospital plunges the boy into despair, and anger – which he vents on the servants, brusquely ordering them to 'Get on with it!' His guilty wish to avoid the unpleasant consequences for a family unable to cope with the invalid turns into a racialist explosion against the only person close enough to him to be his victim: Sam. Sam's attempt to console Hally by evoking the pleasure of dancing, 'like being in a dream about a world in which accidents don't happen', is finally destroyed by the second telephone call. Father is, after all, returning. 'So much for a bloody world without collisions', cries Hally. 'Do you want to know what is really wrong with your lovely little dream, Sam? . . . You left out the cripples'. Reckless with pain, he conjures up an image chillingly reminiscent of the end of *Hello and Goodbye*: 'When you come to think of it, it's a bloody comical sight. I mean, it's bad enough on two legs . . . but one and a pair of crutches!' 'It's a terrible sin for a son to mock his father with jokes like that', urges Sam; but, when Hally repeats an ugly racialist joke told him by his father, about black 'arses', the black man tears off his jacket, drops his trousers, and *presents his backside for Hally's inspection*'. The boy cannot look. Then, when Sam puts a forgiving hand on his shoulder, he turns and spits in his face.

As in the climactic moment of *The Blood Knot* years before, further violence seems imminent. The tension in the theatre at this point is almost unbearable, as Sam resists the natural, expected response. With terrible self-control, he wipes his face, and suggests they 'try again'. He reminds the boy, who sits hunched in agony as he does so, of the time they flew the kite. The young Hally had gone to sit on a bench marked 'Whites Only', not understanding why his friend could not join him there; but things have changed. 'You know what that bench means now, and you can leave it any time you choose. All you've got to do is stand up and walk away from it.' What we have been made to realise is how difficult, if not impossible, that 'all' is. Hally cannot accept the offer of reconciliation, and he stumbles off into the dark, leaving the two black men alone in the tearoom. Willie starts the jukebox. 'Let's dream', he says, and the two join up, and dance slowly to the strains of Sarah Vaughan's *Little Man You're Crying*. The lights dim to dark. We are left with a resonant image of brotherhood, that brotherhood from which the white 'master' has excluded himself.

It is a sad but instructive irony that Sam Semela died in

his poor New Brighton home shortly before John Kani
arrived to take him to see the local, South African premiere
at the Market Theatre in 1983 – in which Kani himself
played the former waiter. For Kani, the role was 'something hard and hurtful' that had to be done 'for a vital lesson
to be learnt'.[6] Yet, like Fugard, he has had to face the
criticism which has been levelled against the play: of
condoning the racial insult and humiliation at its centre.
But, although forgiveness rather than retaliation is offered,
this does not necessarily mean the play is limited to serving
the status quo. Fugard always defuses violence; but he
shows that it is imminent, unless there *is* change. He admits
that his society 'remains as entrenched in all its viciousness
as was the case at any point in the past', despite 'cosmetic'
improvements, such as the desegregation of theatres; yet

> I still believe that theatre is an inordinately civilising
> factor in any society. It does provoke people to think and
> feel, sometimes about things they don't want to think and
> feel. One of my most passionate convictions is that if the
> majority of white South Africans got around to doing
> that, then we should stand some real chance of things
> happening inside that country.[7]

Like other art forms, theatre can only survive if people
believe in it. Fugard does, evidently; and, by giving some of
the issues which touch all of us a local habitation and a
name, he shows the continuing value and relevance of
drama today. But no South African can escape the
corrupting influence of their situation, and he is no
exception. He sees things from the white liberal point of
view, and is unable to avoid that. His most recent plays, *A
Lesson from Aloes* and *'Master Harold' . . . and the boys*,
are obviously about the white experience, and directed in

the first place towards white audiences. This is a long way from the achievement of the *Statements* plays. Yet what remains important is that, in the words of a favourite poet, he still aims to stand 'as witness to the common lot, / survivor of that time, that place' (Anna Akhmatova, 'Requiem'). His testimony is personal, and immediate; what matters to him is the individual experience; and his commitment to that, expressed as a 'living moment' on stage, has, in practice, meant going beyond the limitations of his own position – even, at times, expressing the dissidence of a race and class not his own.

Notes

1. Introduction

1. *Athol Fugard: Notebooks 1960–1977*, ed. Mary Benson (1983) p. 89.

2. Ibid., pp. 77–98. Pound actually defined 'image' as 'that which presents an intellectual and emotional complex in a moment of time'.

3. *Albert Camus: Selected Essays and Notebooks*, ed. and trs. Philip Thody (1970) p. 26; and see Craig Raine, 'An Interview with Athol Fugard', *Quarto*, no. 9 (Aug 1980) 9.

4. *Camus Notebooks*, p. 235; *Fugard Notebooks*, p. 172.

5. Introduction to Olive Schreiner, *The Story of an African Farm* (1971 edn) p. 7.

6. 'Life with a Liberal Conscience' (interview), *Guardian*, 24 July 1971.

7. Athol Fougard (*sic*), 'The Blood Knot' (foreword to an extract), *Contrast* (Cape Town), II, no. 1 (Autumn 1962) 29.

8. Interview with the author, Sardinia Bay, 3 Jan 1982.

9. 'The Impossibility of a Liberal Solution in South Africa', in *The Liberal Dilemma in South Africa*, ed. P. L. van den Berghe (1979) p. 63.

10. 'Athol Fugard at Forty' (interview), *To the Point* (Cape Town), 3 June 1972.

2. Career and Personal Influences

1. 'Interview with Athol Fugard', *News/Check* (Johannesburg), 21 July

1967, p. 24; 'Keeping an Appointment with the Future: the Theatre of Athol Fugard' (interview with Mary Benson), *Theatre Quarterly*, VII, no. 28 (Winter 1977–8) 77.

2. Raine interview, *Quarto*, no. 9, p. 9.

3. Introduction, *'Boesman and Lena' and Other Plays* (1978) p. vii.

4. In conversation with the author, Sardinia Bay, 3 Jan 1982.

5. Unpublished letter, 28 Oct 1953, National English Literary Museum MS 1025/4.

6. Programme note, *Dimetos*, Edinburgh International Festival, 1975; Colin Smith, 'White Man on a Tightrope' (interview), *Observer*, 6 Jan 1974, p. 8.

7. *Fugard Notebooks*, pp. 25–6.

8. Benson interview, *Theatre Quarterly*, VII, no. 28, p. 78.

9. Jonathan Marks, 'Interview with Athol Fugard', *Yale/Theatre*, IV, no. 1 (winter 1973) 72; 'Afrikaner Humanist' (interview), *Observer*, 18 July 1971.

10. In conversation with the author, Sardinia Bay, 3 Jan. 1982.

11. 'Athol Fugard', in *At the Royal Court*, ed. Richard Findlater (1981) p. 160.

3. The Sophiatown Plays

1. 'Nights When *Tsotsi* Was Born', *Rand Daily Mail* (Johannesburg), 11 Feb 1980; Anthony Sampson, *Drum* (1956) p. 228.

2. 'Athol Plans an African Theatre', *Rand Daily Mail*, 17 Sep 1958.

3. 'Mshengu', 'Political Theatre in South Africa and the Work of Athol Fugard', *Theatre Research International*, VII (1982) 173.

4. R. G., 'A European Looks at *No Good Friday* and Finds it Good Theatre', *Zonk* (Johannesburg), Dec 1958.

5. 'Towards an African Theatre', *Rand Daily Mail*, 2 Apr 1981.

6. Benson interview, *Theatre Quarterly*, VII, no. 28, p. 78.

7. 'Diary of a Black Actor', in Jill Johnson and Peter Magubane, *Soweto Speaks* (1981) p. 155.

8. Barrie Hough, 'Interview with Fugard', 30 Nov 1977, repr. in *Athol Fugard*, ed. Stephen Gray (1982) p. 122.

9. Barry Ronge, 'Shedding a New Light on Shebeen Queens', *Star* (Johannesburg), 24 Nov 1981.

10. See, for example, 'Shebeens Never Like This', *Port Elizabeth Herald*, 10 June 1959.

11. Lewis Nkosi, 'Let's Vitalise the Theatre', *Contact* (Cape Town), 27 June 1959.

4. 'Three Port Elizabeth Plays' and 'People Are Living There'

1. Repr. in Fugard's Introduction to *'Boesman and Lena' and Other Plays* (1980) p. ix. I give this version since it is evidently nearer the original than that in the *Fugard Notebooks* (see p. 15).
2. 'The Minotaur or The Stop in Oran' (1939) repr. in *The Myth of Sisyphus* (1976 edn) p. 149.
3. Introduction, *Boesman and Lena*, p. xv (cf. *Fugard Notebooks*, pp. 105–6).
4. Ibid., p. xxiv (cf. *Fugard Notebooks*, p. 174).
5. Letter to Almeda K. Rae, repr. in *Athol Fugard*, p. 51.
6. Interview in *Observer*, 10 July 1971.
7. J. A. Brown, 'SA Theatre at its Finest', *Sunday Times* (Johannesburg), 12 Nov 1961; B. Levin, 'They Really are Blind', *Daily Mail*, 22 Feb 1963; K. Tynan, 'Under the Influence', *Oberver*, 24 Feb 1963.
8. Introduction, *Boesman and Lena*, p. xi.
9. *'Boesman and Lena'*, *New Republic* (New York), 25 July 1970.
10. Introduction, *Boesman and Lena*, p. xxv.

5. The 'Statements' Plays

1. Stanley Kauffmann, *'Sizwe Bansi* and *The Island'*, *New Republic*, 21 Dec 1974; John Elsom, 'The Condemned', *Listener*, 10 Jan 1974.
2. *Fugard Notebooks*, p. 81.
3. As reported by John Kani in conversation with the author, Port Elizabeth, 17 Jan 1982. See also *Fugard Notebooks*, p. 125. I have drawn on my interview with Kani for much of the information about the Serpent Players here.
4. *Guardian* (interview), 8 Jan 1974.
5. *Observer Magazine* (interview), 4 Dec 1983. A full account of this event is given in *A Night at the Theatre*, ed. Ronald Harwood (1983).
6. *Fugard Notebooks*, p. 83.
7. Ibid., pp. 178–9.

6. Man Alone: 'Dimetos' and 'The Guest'

1. *Fugard Notebooks*, p. 223; A. C. Tucker, 'Athol Fugard' (interview), *Transatlantic Review*, no. 53/4 (Feb 1976) 87.
2. Hough interview, repr. in *Athol Fugard*, p. 128; *Fugard Notebooks*, p. 222; Benson interview, *Theatre Quarterly*, VII, no. 28, p. 83.

7. Port Elizabeth Revisited: 'Marigolds', 'Aloes' and ' "Master Harold" . . . and the boys'

1. *Fugard Notebooks*, p. 183.

2. Ibid., p. 207.

3. Quoted in Denis Herbstein, *White Man, We Want to Talk to You* (1978) p. 68.

4. 'A Protest before our Very Eyes', *Sunday Times*, 13 July 1980.

5. Interview with Paul Alan, *Kaleidoscope* (BBC Radio 4), 25 Jan 1984.

6. 'Harold's "Boy" Sees Role as Duty' (interview), *Argus* (Cape Town), 29 Sep 1983.

7. *Kaleidoscope* interview, 25 Jan 1984.

Bibliography

(i) Works by Athol Fugard

PLAYS

The Blood Knot (Johannesburg: Simondium, 1963; New York: Odyssey, 1963; New York: Samuel French, 1969; London and Cape Town: Oxford University Press, Three Crowns, 1974), included in *Penguin English Dramatists 13* (Harmondsworth: Penguin, 1968).

People Are Living There (Cape Town: Buren, 1969; London and Cape Town: Oxford University Press, Three Crowns, 1970).

Boesman and Lena (Cape Town: Buren, 1969; London and Cape Town: Oxford University Press, Three Crowns, 1970; New York: Samuel French, 1972).

Hello and Goodbye (Cape Town: Balkema, 1971; New York: Samuel French, 1971; London and Cape Town: Oxford University Press, Three Crowns, 1973).

'The Coat' and 'The Third Degree' [by Don MacLennan]: *Two Experiments in Playmaking* (Cape Town: Balkema, 1971).

Three Port Elizabeth Plays, including *The Blood Knot, Hello and Goodbye* and *Boesman and Lena* (London: Oxford University Press, 1974; New York: Viking, 1974).

Statements: Two Workshop Productions Devised by Athol Fugard, John Kani, and Winston Ntshona: 'Sizwe Bansi Is Dead' and 'The Island'; and a New Play: 'Statements after an Arrest under the Immorality Act' (London: Oxford University Press, 1974).

Bibliography

'*Sizwe Bansi Is Dead*' *and 'The Island*' (New York: Viking, 1976).
'*Dimetos' and Two Early Plays*, including *Nongogo* and *No-Good Friday* (London: Oxford University Press, 1977).
'*Boesman and Lena' and Other Plays*, including *The Blood Knot, People Are Living There* and *Hello and Goodbye* (London and Cape Town: Oxford University Press, 1978, 1980).
Orestes, as a letter describing the performance, in *Theatre One: New South African Drama*, ed. Stephen Gray (Johannesburg: Donker, 1978).
A Lesson from Aloes (Oxford and New York: Oxford University Press, 1981).
'*Master Harold' ... and the boys* (Oxford and New York: Oxford University Press, 1983).

FILM SCRIPTS

The Occupation, in *Ten One-Act Plays*, ed. Cosmo Pieterse (London: Heinemann Educational, 1968).
The Guest: An Episode in the Life of Eugene Marais, with Ross Devenish (Johannesburg: Donker, 1977).
Marigolds in August (Johannesburg: Donker, 1982).
[The script of *Mille Miglia* ('Theatre 625', BBC2, 5 Aug 1965) is unpublished.]

NON-DRAMATIC WORKS

Tsotsi (Johannesburg: Donker, 1980; London: Rex Collings, 1980; New York: Random House, 1980; Harmondsworth: Penguin, 1983).
Notebooks: 1960–1977, ed. Mary Benson (Johannesburg: Donker, 1983; London and Boston, Mass.: Faber and Faber, 1983).

(ii) Selected Criticism and Background

Athol Fugard, ed. Stephen Gray (Johannesburg: McGraw-Hill, 1982): the only relevant book-length work: an anthology of interviews, reviews and critical essays, plus detailed bibliography.
Benson, Mary, 'Athol Fugard and "One Little Corner of the World"', *Yale/Theatre*, IV, no. 1 (Winter 1973) 55–62.
——, 'Keeping an Appointment with the Future', *Theatre Quarterly*, VII, no. 28 (Winter 1977–8) 77–83. This issue contains a number of relevant articles.
'Black Theatre in South Africa', *International Defence and Aid Fact Paper*, no. 2 (June 1976).

Bibliography

Brecht, Bertolt, *The Messingkauf Dialogues*, trs. J. Willett (London: Methuen, 1965).

Brook, Peter, *The Empty Space* (Harmondsworth: Penguin, 1978).

Camus, Albert, *The Myth of Sisyphus* (Harmondsworth: Penguin, 1975).

——, *Selected Essays and Notebooks*, ed. and trs. Philip Thody (Harmondsworth: Penguin, 1970).

Coveney, M., 'Challenging the Silence' (interview), *Plays and Players*, XXI, no. 2 (Nov 1973) 34–7; repr. in *Index*, III, no. 1 (1974) 85–8. *Index* has regular items on the state of censorship in South Africa.

Gray, Stephen, *Southern African Literature: An Introduction* (Cape Town and London: Philip/Collings, 1979).

Green, Robert J., 'The Drama of Athol Fugard', in *Aspects of South African Literature*, ed. C. Heywood (London: Heinemann, 1976) pp. 163–73.

Grotowski, Jerzy, *Towards a Poor Theatre* (London: Methuen, 1969).

Gussow, Mel, 'Profile: Witness' (Athol Fugard), *New Yorker*, 20 Dec 1982, pp. 47–94.

Herbstein, Denis, *White Man, We Want to Talk to You* (Harmondsworth: Penguin, 1978).

The Liberal Dilemma in South Africa, ed. P. L. van den Berghe (London: Croom Helm, 1979).

Marks, Jonathan, 'Interview with Athol Fugard', *Yale/Theatre*, IV, no. 1 (Winter 1973) 64–72.

'Mshengu' (Robert MacLaren or Kavanagh), 'Political Theatre in South Africa and the Work of Athol Fugard', *Theatre Research International*, VII (1982) 160–79.

O'Sheel, Patrick, 'Athol Fugard's "Poor Theatre"', *Journal of Commonwealth Literature*, XII (Apr 1978) 67–77.

Raine, Craig, 'An Interview with Athol Fugard', *Quarto*, no. 9 (Aug 1980) 9–14.

Sepamla, Sipho, 'Towards an African Theatre', *Rand Daily Mail*, 2 Apr 1981.

Walder, Dennis, *Selected Plays of Fugard* (London and Beirut: Longman York Notes, 1980).

Weales, G., 'The Embodied Images of Athol Fugard', *Hollins Critic*, XV, no. 1 (Feb 1978) 1–2.

Index

actors: Fugard's debt to, 9; *see also* individual names
Adams, Perseus, 21
Aeschylus, 6
African Music and Drama Association, 1, 45–6
African National Congress, 15, 35, 56, 76
African Theatre Workshop, 24, 29
Afrikaner Nationalist Party, 14
Akhmatova, Anna, 'Requiem', 126
Amorous Prawn, The, 2
Anouilh, Jean, 76
Antigone (Sophocles), 6, 75–6, 80–1, 88–90
apartheid: psychological effects of, 2–3; divisiveness of, 8; social effects of, 13–17; and surplus work force, 39; *Statements* plays and, 76, 87

Ardrey, Robert, 106
Artaud, Antonin, 4
Astbury, Brian, 28–9
Astbury, Yvonne *see* Bryceland, Yvonne

BBC TV, 26, 28, 69, 98
Bannen, Ian, 26, 61
Beck, Julian, 83
Beckett, Samuel, 9, 25, 55; *Waiting for Godot*, 55
Bernhardt, Ian, 45
Berry, John, 26
Biko, Steve, 15, 112
Black Women's Federation, 99
Blood Knot, The: first performed, 1–2, 46; and Fugard's 'witness', 6; impact of, 11–12, 25–6; and Fugard's interest in cars, 21; genesis of, 24–5; Serpent Players and, 30; action in,

Index

Index